C000120958

Rejection, Resist
Resurrection
Speaking out on racism in the church

MUKTI BARTON

To treat a child of God as if he or she was less than this is not just wrong, which it is; it is not just evil, as it often is; not just painful, as it often must be for the victim; it is veritably blasphemous, for it is to spit in the face of God.

Archbishop Desmond Tutu

DARTON·LONGMAN+TODD

I dedicate this book
to my multicultured family:

    my husband, Stephen
    and our two sons Richard Sumitro and Matthew Krishanu.

        My family is a living parable
        of a loving community
        which fights against
        injustices of many different kinds.

First published in 2005 by
Darton, Longman and Todd Ltd
1 Spencer Court
140–142 Wandsworth High Street
London SW18 4JJ

ISBN 0 232 52612 5

A catalogue record for this book is available from the British Library.

Designed by Sandie Boccacci
Phototypeset in 9.5/12pt Palatino by
Intype Libra Ltd
Printed and bound in Great Britain by
Page Bros, Norwich, Norfolk

Contents

Acknowledgements

First of all, I am greatly indebted to all who entrusted me with their stories. I am especially grateful to the Black and Asian Network Core Group members who played an active part in bringing this book about: Mrs Ruth Alleyne, Mrs Marjorie Bartley, Mrs Joney Blair, Mrs Sylvette Brown, Mrs Mildred Browne, Mrs Heather Carty, Mrs Evadne Christian, Ms Mona Contractor, Mrs Noreen Gross, Mrs Josephine Henry, Mr Vanico James, Mrs Jacquie Jones, Mr Aubrey Longe, the Revd Isaiah Phillip, Mrs Patricia Brown-Richards, Mr Kevin Thompson and above all to Mr Tony Kelly who first proposed the writing of this book. Many of the group gave their own stories and collected others'. They constantly encouraged and enthused me to fulfil the task.

I am thankful to the Diocesan Centenary Planning Group for acknowledging the importance of this book; the director of Ministries Forum, the Revd Canon Dr Brian Russell for allowing me to make the writing of the book the priority in the centenary year; the Revd Dr David Hewlett, the principal of Queen's Foundation for Ecumenical Theological Education, for giving me study leave; my two colleagues at Queen's Foundation, the Revd Dr Michael Jagessar and Dr Anthony Reddie for covering my work during my study leave; and my diocesan colleague Ms Andrea Stevens for transcribing stories from the dictaphones.

I am especially grateful to the Bishop for the Diocese of Birmingham, the Rt Revd Dr John Sentamu (shortly to become the Archbishop of York), for writing the foreword. He will launch this book in Birmingham Cathedral on 3 September 2005 so that attention is drawn to Racial Justice Sunday, which is always the second Sunday in September. It is particularly significant that this book is written during the episcopate of Bishop Sentamu, who was one of the Advisers who supported Sir William Macpherson in writing the Stephen Lawrence Enquiry Report after the murder of Stephen Lawrence, a Black young man who was killed simply because of his colour. As a follow up to the enquiry report Bishop Sentamu urged the churches to become conscious of institutional racism from within. At present he is playing a prominent role in the 'Make

Poverty History' campaign. The bishop constantly demonstrates that a church faithful to Christ cannot but work towards social transformation until the Kingdom of God comes on earth.

I thank Mr Tony Kelly and my husband Stephen for reading the full manuscript and offering helpful comments and suggestions.

I also wish to thank the following for their kind permission to reproduce copyright material: Vilma Jarrett-Harvey, Linda Jones, Janet Johnson, Sharon Palmer, and Nicola Slee for their poems; SPCK, also for Nicola Slee's poem; Asian Women's Resource Centre for Culture and Theology in Malaysia for extracts from their publications; Wild Goose Publications for an extract from their publication.

It has been great working with my editor, Virginia Hearn, and all the team at Darton, Longman and Todd.

Foreword

I welcome this book as a set of stories that are offered on behalf of many Christians and Anglicans from minority ethnic groups. The stories are a powerful reminder of the past and a timely challenge to the present. People speak movingly of their deep faith, bringing their hurts before God for healing, and witnessing to a faith in the God who loves, includes and desires to bring all people to new life through the risen Christ. There is a proper way in which Christians, from their experience of rejection, can take responsibility under Christ to be agents of change and transformation. Through this, the powerful grace and forgiving love of God can be at work to bring us towards a resurrection, a new life as we grow into God's Kingdom. These stories express this solid hope that comes through struggle and through a deep attachment to God.

It is important to place these stories in a wider context. The Stephen Lawrence Inquiry into the death of Stephen Lawrence highlighted the way in which there are ways of working, structures of organisation, patterns of attitudes, that can pervade an institution. This shapes the actions and behaviour of the individuals who inhabit that institution. In the Inquiry Report we grappled with the problem of institutional racism and taking all that we heard in evidence and read we said:

> For the purposes of our Inquiry the concept of institutional racism which we apply consists of:
>
> **The collective failure of an organisation to provide an appropriate and professional service to people because of their colour, culture, or ethnic origin. It can be seen or detected in processes, attitudes and behaviour which amount to discrimination through unwitting prejudice, ignorance, thoughtlessness and racist stereotyping which disadvantage minority ethnic people.**
>
> It persists because of the failure of the organisation openly and adequately to recognise and address its existence and causes by policy, example and leadership. Without recogni-

tion and action to eliminate such racism it can prevail as part of the ethos or culture of the organisation. It is a corrosive disease.
(The Stephen Lawrence Inquiry Report, Paragraph 6.34, p. 28, February 1999)

The stories that follow in this book speak of the pain of what it is to undergo these kinds of institutional racism. The cost is in terms of the lives of people who are hampered in their growth into the image of God created in them. These kinds of institutional racism are in society and so inevitably (to some degree) found in the churches, both in the Church of England and other churches. The stories which follow voice these concerns for those in many different churches. It is as we attend to these stories, that we can deepen our mutual love and understanding. This can lead us to join together in ways that liberate us all to be more fully like Christ. This is good news indeed!

I am glad that this book is offered through the Diocese of Birmingham in this Centenary year. The Diocese has sought to tackle these issues in a variety of thoughtful ways over recent years. The stories that follow pay tribute, for example, to the pioneering work of Paul Burrough as the Bishop's Chaplain, to the work of clergy like John Wilkinson in Aston, and to the study courses provided by the Diocese. The post of Bishop's Adviser was created by Bishop Hugh, and Dr Mukti Barton is the third holder of this post. The Diocese took very seriously the *Seeds of Hope* course, which was intended to bring to light ways that we can change to grow more fully into mutual love. The stories that follow highlight the positive impact that this course had in parishes. My predecessor, Bishop Mark, undertook a review of the structures of the Diocese to look for ways in which those from minority ethnic groups can be more included. This highlighted the importance of diocesan courses in theology and the stories that follow often pay tribute to these inspirational courses. I am so glad that in this Centenary year there are more members from minority ethnic groups taking up membership of diocesan committees than ever before, and a good number exploring ministries of various kinds. This is a great encouragement for the future.

The pathway for people from minority ethnic groups has been particularly hard. The people who came from the Caribbean had a double diaspora in their cultural histories – the dislocation caused by the uprooting from Africa and into slavery and then the second diaspora as they met and experienced British society in the 1950s and 1960s. The stories show that Christians from cultures like South Asia also had a hard pathway – British people finding it hard to imagine that it is possible to be Asian and a Christian, rather than someone of a different world faith. The stories that follow give the inside account of what this has meant in personal terms. In a brave way, the speakers take us behind the scenes into their spiritual biographies. This calls for our respect.

In Birmingham, we are constantly aware of a variety of stories. Our Diocese includes the many urban areas and estates on the (then) perimeter of the city built over the last fifty years. Here too there are experiences of being poor and on the margins, of feeling despair and hopelessness. This is often the seedbed for overt White racism in British society. This book shows how healing must come through ways of including all people and, as these speakers often say, bringing us from competition and scapegoating and into the love of Christ that enables us all to rise above our past attitudes.

Finally, I feel strengthened by the themes of hope that emerge through these stories. The local church has, for all its weaknesses, been for many people a place of support and nurture that has helped them when meeting racism in their daily lives. Family life has been a nest or cradle of faith and identity that has given people a sense of worth and the reality of being people who belong to God. Through all this our Lord Jesus Christ, that great Shepherd of the sheep, can be sensed as a God who beckons and equips us for a new future, with one whole human race meeting to celebrate new life in God's Kingdom. The same Jesus who bears those wounds has led us on a path so that we can begin to share even now in his risen life. Those who tell their stories in this book have a deep knowledge of this Jesus.

The Rt Revd Dr John Sentamu
Bishop for the Diocese of Birmingham
Trinity Sunday 2005

Introduction

A Psalm for All Who Keep God's Word
Blessed are we who are doers of the word,
who hear God's word
and keep it.

One thing alone does God require
and this do we seek to accomplish:
to do justice,
to love tenderly,
to walk humbly
with our God.

Blessed are we who are doers of the word,
who hear God's word
and keep it.

Who heal the brokenhearted
and bind the wounds of the oppressed,
feed the hungry,
shelter the homeless,
set the imprisoned free:
these are God's disciples,
God's family,
God's friends.

Blessed are we who are doers of the word,
who hear God's word
and keep it.

The word of God is a two-edged sword
that cuts through all hypocrisy,
prunes the unsuspecting,
strikes at the root of evil,
pierces the heart.

Blessed are we who are doers of the word,
who hear God's word
and keep it.

The word of God is a lamp to our feet,
a lantern to our path,
the light of the world
crying out for a sign
of hope
and illumination.

Blessed are we who are doers of the word,
who hear God's word
and keep it.

The word of God is a spark of life
living among the rubble,
igniting a global consciousness
to ways we are one world only,
a beacon burning
deep in the hearts
of those who seek justice
and peace.

Blessed are we who are doers of the word,
who hear God's word
and keep it.

The word of God is the word made flesh
in every generation,
in the outcasts of the system,
on the margins of prestige and power,
on the downside of tradition,
in every face
and every place
where God's own Spirit dwells.

Blessed are we who are doers of the word,
who hear God's word
and keep it.

Blessed are all who love God's word
and live it to the full,
for they are like trees
by rippling streams,
birds that sore high,
singing,
prophets of a new age
bringing
the Good News
to all.

Blessed are we who are doers of the word,
who hear God's word
and keep it.[1]

Author unknown

This book offers insight into the real experiences of Black and Asian Christians today. It does so for the most part in their own words, with the tones and inflections of their voices. Their voice is strong, because they speak of their own history, their concrete life experience and not about abstract concepts. Black people tell of a truth that they have known in that 'most sensitive receiver for historical reality', their bodies. 'They remember what it is like to be a *no-body* and what it is like to be a *some-body*. The power of their storytelling lies in its embodied truth.'[2]

> There is no truth for and about black people that does not emerge out of the context of their experience. Truth in this sense is black truth, a truth disclosed in the history and culture of black people ... It is an investigation of the mind into the raw materials of our pilgrimage, telling the story of 'how we got over'.[3]

In April 2004, during a meeting of the Birmingham Diocesan Black and Asian Network Core Group, Mr Tony Kelly suggested to the group that we record our stories of life in the Church of England. The year 2005 is Birmingham Diocesan Centenary and all the people present immediately recognised the *kairos*, the decisive epoch waited for.[4] People wanted to explore the raw materials of their pilgrimage, telling the story of 'how we got over'.

The term 'we' needs explanation. In Birmingham, Black and

Asian Anglicans have bonded together and we as a Network Core Group meet at least six times a year. A larger Network Group that meets twice a year has a membership of over three hundred people. These groups are caucuses, but not exclusive. At every Network event members are invited to come along with other people. The caucuses present the voice of Black people and nobody is barred from hearing it. According to Barbara Findlay, 'When we organize things we should expect and encourage caucuses around different constellations of oppression and dominance ... we need to under-stand that caucuses are part of a process of coming to voice.'[5] Our experience proved Findlay's observation to be right. Caucuses are indeed part of a process of coming to voice. Without Black caucuses this book would not have been written.

In this book Black Anglicans have spoken out on racism in church. The term racism needs qualifying before I proceed any further. David Haslam understands

> racism as a kind of corporate poison, like something in the water, or the air, by which everyone is affected. It invades the mind gradually, sometimes not giving any signs of being present until triggered off by a particular set of circumstances. It may create hallucinations of pleasantness and well being. It is present in all White people, even though some struggle against it ... Ubiquitous, the poison is very difficult to remove, and can certainly not be eradicated by a one-off 'surgical operation'.[6]

This poisonous air has not always been in the world. Many different kinds of prejudices are around and they all need to be castigated, but this book is about a particular kind of prejudice, which is racism. The term 'race' originated in the early sixteenth century,[7] and in the later years the idea of 'race' began to get respectability.

> Enlightenment philosophy was instrumental in codifying and institutionalizing both the scientific and popular European per-ceptions of the human race. The numerous writings on race by Hume, Kant, and Hegel played a strong role in articu-lating Europe's sense not only of its cultural but also *racial* superiority. In their writings ... 'reason' and 'civilization' became almost synonymous with 'white' people and northern Europe, while unreason and savagery were conveniently

located among the non-whites, the 'black', the 'red', the 'yellow', outside Europe.[8]

European philosophers divided peoples into various 'races' and accorded a hierarchical order to them. These thinkers were not in agreement about how many 'races' there should be and what they were, but they were all certain about conferring the top place of the hierarchy to White people.[9]

'Did race prejudice cause slavery? Or was it the other way round? Winthrop D. Jordan ... argues that prejudice and slavery may well have been equally cause and effect.'[10] Before slavery, colour prejudice already existed in Europe. During slavery and colonialism this prejudice was turned into a racist ideology for political and economic gain. The pseudo-scientific theories of Johann Friedrich Blumenbach, 'father of craniology or phrenology', were greatly utilised by European scholars to give respectability to racist ideologies.

> He [Blumenbach] collected human skulls from all over the world, and it was one of these skulls, from the Caucasus in Russia, that led him to suppose that Europeans came from that region, to coin the word 'Caucasian' to describe the white variety of humans, and to prefer this 'most beautiful form of the skull'.[11]

Craniology or phrenology has long been discredited and proved to be unscientific,[12] yet many White people still define themselves as Caucasian. Confusingly, Blumenbach also included some Asians and Africans in the Caucasian category and excluded some Europeans.[13] It is an irony that when reason and civilization became synonymous with White people, they produced the most unreasonable, inconsistent, irrational and unscientific race theories. These theories are now outdated, yet White people, who were always put on the top of the racial hierarchy, still tend to give an impression that they are superior to all others.

> Racism is a product of the belief of racial superiority derived from the British colonial past and the history of the slave trade, embedded in the institutions of British Society and is manifested in the institutional and personal practices of the White majority through conscious and unconscious discrimination against and oppression of Black and minority ethnic people.[14]

Many Christians find the issue of racism in the church an

uncomfortable one but it is a well-known fact that for centuries western Christianity accommodated racism, colonialism and slavery. The Revd Canon John Wilkinson asks:

> How did English Christianity, and in particular the Church of England, respond to slavery and racism? Since the Church of England was most bound up with the ruling classes, its involvement with slavery is deeper, more thorough and longer-lasting than that of other denominations.[15]

Dr Robert Beckford might be right in claiming that church and racism are married to each other; they are bedfellows.[16] It is significant that many White supremacist racist groups have chosen the church's emblem, the cross, as their symbol. The cross, or a Celtic cross, is the emblem of several racist skinhead groups, including Stormfront; various Klan organisations use a cross with a blood drop at the centre; and the violently anti-Jewish *Posse Comitatus* also incorporates a cross in its badge. Some such groups name themselves as churches, such as the notorious World Church of the Creator.[17]

Race theories contradict the very essence of the Bible and of Christianity. God did not create many races, but one race, the human race. All human beings are created in God's own image (Gen. 1:27). 'From one ancestor he made all nations to inhabit the whole earth', says Paul (Acts. 17:26).[18] When human beings corrupted God's world order, Jesus broke down all the barriers and heralded a new creation. 'There is no longer Jew or Greek, there is no longer slave or free, there is no longer male and female; for all of you are one in Christ Jesus' (Gal. 3:28). In this book Black Anglicans are trying to make the church 'relinquish its marriage to racism'[19] and urging White people to join them in their struggle. This struggle is more difficult for White people because racism bestows on them power over Black people. Relinquishing power and privilege is not an easy task for any human group.

This power dynamic makes racism a political category and the term Black a political term. Although written in 1996 David Haslam's discussion is still helpful:

> Overall, just as racism is a political category, 'Black' is primarily a political colour ... Most activists in the field from the minority communities still seem most often to use 'black', seeing it as a political description which includes all who are the objects of racism ... Those from these communities who are less

happy to use 'Black' sometimes use 'Black and Asian' ...
Another option is to use 'black and minority ethnic' as the
adjective, on the basis that all of us are 'ethnic' communities,
including white British, and in Britain certain groups are in the
minority ... When using 'minority' however, it is important to
remember that ... in the world as a whole (as increasingly in the
Christian Churches) white people are a pretty small
minority ... The North American 'catch-all' phrase is 'people of
colour'. That does not seem to have caught on in the UK.[20]

As racism is complex, so is discussion of the terms Black and
White. 'The term white has been used to refer to the skin colour of
Europeans or people of European extraction since the early 17th
century.'[21] However, it is good to remember that White is also a
political term. A Spanish woman who has been a victim of racism in
the UK recently told me that she is not White. In the context of the
USA Abby L. Ferber writes: 'The Irish were ... once considered non-
white in the United States, and US racial categories change with
almost every census.'[22]

I will refer to Black and White people with upper case B and W
to indicate that these are not simply adjectives describing people's
skin-colour. 'Black with upper case B has tended to be used to refer
to Black as a proudly chosen identity, history and culture associ-
ated with African roots, distinguishing the term from a simple
adjective 'black' describing colour.'[23] 'Black' will be generally used
to include Asians, but when it is appropriate I will adopt the term
'Black and Asian'. Moreover, separate chapters are dedicated to
accounts of the distinct forms of racism Asian Christians suffer.

After centuries of oppression because of their skin colour, in the
1960s, during the Civil Rights and Black Power movements, the
Black consciousness era began in America. 'As Black youngsters
strutted the streets clothed in "Blackness" they often shouted the
words of a popular song during that era, "Say it loud, I'm Black and
I am Proud!"'[24] This movement has given voice to non-White people
of the world and many are now proudly calling themselves Black in
order to counteract racism. As long as racism exists and the world
remains divided on colour lines the terms Black and White will
have to be applied.

Peter Fryer reminds us, 'There were Africans in Britain before
the Anglo-Saxons came here.' The Africans were soldiers in the
Roman imperial army.[25] However, in recent years more Black people
have come. In the 1950s and 1960s there was a labour shortage and

Black and Asian people were invited to come to live and work in Britain. When the newcomers, many of whom were Anglicans, arrived they found signs of White superiority and racism everywhere. But most shocking for them was the experience of rejection in the Anglican churches. They were part of the Anglican Communion, yet they experienced various forms of rejection on account of their skin colour.

Black people had to dig deep inside themselves to find the strength that only God can give. They resisted racism and survived. Now they can tell stories of resurrection. People who were rejected have become the cornerstone holding up many churches in Birmingham. The Anglican Church, which 'took some two hundred years before it recognised that African peoples, or Amerindian peoples had souls that could be saved',[26] is now globally a Black majority church. 'The stone that the builders rejected has become the cornerstone; this was the Lord's doing' (Matt. 21:42).

However, Black people still experience rejection in the Church of England. Racism is persistent. Black Anglicans find their strength from their deep Christian faith and by networking with each other. Black and Asian Liberation Theology helps them to make sense of their experience and empowers them in their belief that they are created beautifully in God's own image. They remain with their White brothers and sisters in Christ and continue to worship and minister within the church they love and to which they belong. Their experiences expose the incompatibility of racism and Christianity. Yet White Christians who perpetrate racism are usually unaware of the part they play in keeping racism intact. The narratives in this book expound the pervasiveness and the subtlety of racism.

Various methods were applied to collect stories. A particular Network event was organised to hear Black and Asian people's experience in the Anglican Church. About sixty people attended the event. Four speakers told their stories which were recorded on dictaphones and transcribed. Two Black female poets from other denominations recited some of their poems and offered more of their work for inclusion here. I have used theirs and other, mainly Black and Asian, poets' work in between chapters to link the different voices. At the Network event everybody present had a chance to express something of his or her experience through creative workshops. Such briefer recollections and comments have also been incorporated into the text.

Besides the Network members, Black and Asian people in all

the churches in Birmingham Diocese were invited to tell their stories. Not all could be included, but they provide the general background for the book and show that the accounts published here are not isolated incidents. Stories were collected through interviews during which some Network Core Group members and I took notes. Other people sent their contributions in written form. Some of the storytellers have given their real names and others pen names. I have tried my best not to misinterpret them, and after working with each story I have returned it to the contributor to check that I have not misrepresented them.

These stories therefore largely focus on the Anglican churches in Birmingham, but relevant experiences from other churches in Britain have also been incorporated. Moreover, people's experience of racism in the church is juxtaposed with their experience in society, since Black Christians have to resist racism both inside and outside the church.

The personal stories are interwoven with biblical study and theological reflection. Black and Asian liberation theological insights are applied to set the subject in a broad theological context. Theology is God-talk and Black and Asian theology is these people's God-talk. However, this God-talk is very much about liberation. In the 1960s and 1970s several colonised countries became independent and this newly gained freedom enabled the previously colonised groups to see themselves and other groups in a new light. This is the period when women, Black people and poor people all over the world began to use social sciences to understand their group reality better. This era gave birth to secular movements such as feminism, Black power and civil rights movements, and many other group movements. People began to articulate how 'patriarchy, capitalism, militarism, sexism, racism, classism, religio-cultural ideologies and other "structures" work in isolation or else in complex concert to initiate or aggravate the suffering of persons'.[27]

These secular movements had their theological and spiritual counterparts including Liberation Theology, Feminist Theology, Black and Asian Theology. These theologies can be grouped as theologies of liberation. James Cone, known as 'the father of Black Theology', claims that 'Christianity is essentially a religion of liberation. The function of theology is that of analyzing the meaning of that liberation for the oppressed so they know that their struggle for political, social, and economic justice is consistent with the gospel of Jesus Christ.'[28] It is a common experience of oppressed people, as the incidents of racism in the book also illustrate, that when Christians are not actively involved in the struggle against oppression, they unwittingly perpetuate the oppression of fellow human beings. The stories tell of various strategies of resistance to racism adopted by Black people.

The primary reflection in the book is theological, but in order to analyse the psychology of racism in all its forms, references are made to socio-psychological, socio-political and historical literature of Black and Asian authors. Moreover, insights from White people's literature are included to demonstrate that some White people too are committed to ending racism. Relevant sources support people's particular experiences and these particular stories contribute to the wider global discussion. The bibliography provides a wonderful opportunity for readers to learn more about the intricacies of racism so that they become better equipped to struggle against this deadly poison.

It has been extremely painful for people to speak about their negative experience in the church. Yet they have spoken out primarily for the sake of their posterity. Dr Anthony Reddie affirms how the narratives of forebears might assist future generations: 'Through exposure to the narratives and expressions of faith of their forebears, black children gain access to survival strategies and aphoristic wisdom that might assist them in their individual struggles.'[29]

Stories also have a healing power which Desmond Tutu, the retired Archbishop of Cape Town in South Africa, has described. When people told their stories to the Truth and Reconciliation Commission, Tutu noted:

> Telling their stories did mean you were running the risk of opening wounds, but in fact often they were wounds that had been festering and to open them now in this fashion had the chance of cleansing them and pouring a balm, an ointment on them.[30]

My husband Stephen and I were at a gathering where a White clergyman in Birmingham Diocese expressed his anxiety about the book I was writing. He said: 'After many years healing has taken place among the Black people in our congregation. We are worried that your book will bring out the pain again.' My husband gave an appropriate answer: 'If pain surfaces, it will mean that more healing is needed. If there has been real healing, no pain will surface.'

Many churches ignore festering wounds because they lack the

courage to open up wounds to heal them. Prophet Jeremiah has stern warnings against unjust social orders where wounds are carelessly treated: 'from the least to the greatest everyone is greedy for unjust gain; from prophet to priest everyone deals falsely. They have treated the wound of my people carelessly, saying, "Peace, peace," when there is no peace' (Jer. 8:10–11; see also Jer. 6:14). Through their storytelling Black people have opened up their wounds. We do not know whether there will be any chance of cleansing them and pouring a balm, an ointment on them, but at least the wounds will be aired. The hope is that opening wounds and airing them will help the healing process. Tutu went on to say:

> I don't know why we should have been surprised at the healing potency of story telling. After all, as people of faith we belong in a story-telling community. We have been integrated into the community that tells the story of a God who brought a rabble of slaves out of bondage and led them through the desert into the Promised Land, and they commemorated it all in a feast, a festival, the Passover. We continued the saga in the story of a young man who died on a cross and on the night before he died established a meal as a memorial and we have been telling this story and its sequel ever since.[31]

Jesus rose from the dead, showing that the very cross of oppression could be turned into the vehicle of resurrection and of new hope. The risen Christ appeared to his disciples. Even after the resurrection the marks of the wounds had remained and Jesus showed them to his disciples, asking Thomas even to touch his wounds. Jesus did not flinch from opening his wounds; Black people in this book have not either:

> You were not ashamed of your wounds.
> You showed them to Thomas
> as marks of your ordeal and death.
> I will no longer hide these wounds of mine.
> I will bear them gracefully.
> They tell a resurrection story.[32]

The opening of wounds is a courageous act and so it is to view the wound. When the risen Christ appeared, the disciples had to look at the wounds of oppression for which they were partly responsible, at least by their sin of omission. Instead of standing by Jesus, most of them fled from the scene of Jesus' trial and his crucifixion.

In this book Black and Asian people have opened their

wounds, the wounds that tell resurrection stories. They are inviting the readers to see and touch the wounds so that they too experience something of the pain of brokenness and the joy of resurrection. This book is not recommended as bedtime reading, but some of the poems used are like prayers. I hope they will enable readers to keep going through the more difficult parts. I recommend putting the book down if it is emotionally too uncomfortable and picking it up again another time. There is some connection between the chapters; yet each chapter is independent. Church groups can take chapters from the book to reflect on.

As a guest lecturer in the United States of America Desmond Tutu wondered what wounds might be healed if the USA had a Truth and Reconciliation Commission of its own, if they had the courage to look at the wounds of people in their own society. What Tutu said to them is equally applicable to the people in the UK: 'You are going to become a very strong and wonderful country the day you have the courage to listen to each other.'[33]

1
Motherland, Here I Come

Mother Land
They asked us to come to Mother Land
They didn't tell us snow would burn our hands

They said the streets were paved with gold
They didn't say it would be so cold

They said there's plenty of work for us to do
They never said we'd have to clean their loos

They said we could come and go as we please
They never said our passports we had to leave

They said we are all part of the same human race
They never said their behaviour would be a disgrace

They said that we are all the same
They never said they would make fun of our children's names

They said we would get good health care
They never said we would have to live in fear

They said we would get a good career
They never said we would have to break down barriers

They said our children they would educate
They never said that teacher would discriminate

They said lots of money we would generate
But now they say we must repatriate.[1]

Vilma Jarrett-Harvey

There was a saying, 'The sun never sets on the British empire.' Britain had colonies all over the world and somewhere the sun was always shining in a country which was part of the British empire. Britain was the glorified motherland and people in the colonies were made to feel privileged to belong to Britain as its children. 'The 1948 Nationality Act ... granted United Kingdom citizenship to citizens of Britain's colonies and former colonies. Their British passports gave them the right to come to Britain and stay here for the rest of their lives.'[2] When Mr Henry Brotherson arrived in London on Monday 29 August 1955 he was coming to his motherland. Caribbean people did look to England as their motherland. Ms Millicent Kelly told us that when she came to England from Jamaica in the early 1950s she was excited about going 'home' to the mother country to train as a nurse.

Henry came to England from St Kitts in the Caribbean where he worked for the British Government as a Ranger from 1946 to 1955. He decided to make the journey after reading a newspaper sent to him by a former employee who had come to work in the UK. Almost every page was filled with vacancies for labouring jobs, paying twice as much as Henry was earning as a Ranger. Moreover, all the things advertised in the British newspaper were cheaper than they were in St Kitts. There was a labour shortage and the motherland was looking to the colonies for cheap labour while the colonies were looking to Britain for a better standard of living. The late Michael Manley, former Jamaican Prime Minister, wrote:

> All economic relations in an empire flow from colony to centre and back. There is almost no exchange in an economic sense between the different colonies themselves even when they form part of a region, as is the case with the West Indian Islands.[3]

This colonial pattern continued in the 1950s 'because of the previous lack of British investment which had virtually destroyed the West Indian economy'.[4] Under these circumstances it made complete sense for Henry to want to come to Britain. It was not an easy decision to leave behind his wife and five children, but after consultation with them he decided to resign his post and take the plunge.

He arrived on the Monday in London and went straight to Manchester because he had a friend there. On Tuesday he went with his friend to the Labour Exchange to register. On Thursday he went back to check whether there was a job for him and was told to come back after a few days. On the same day he went in search of the Anglican vicar in the parish. Henry knocked on the vicarage door, introduced himself and was asked in. He gave the vicar a letter he had from the priest of his parish in St Kitts. After reading it the vicar realised that Henry had been a very valuable member in his church. He had been a server, Sunday school teacher, Lay Reader, and a lay representative to the synod. The vicar said that he would be glad to have someone like Henry in his church. He was about to attend a Mothers' Union meeting and told Henry that he would be delighted if Henry could go with him and tell the women something about the Caribbean. Henry went with the vicar, introduced himself and told them about his life in St Kitts.

After the talk the women gathered around him, shook his hand and said that they hoped that Henry would join them in the church. They welcomed him with open arms. Henry went back to his flat feeling happy to have met a parish willing to welcome him. On Sunday Henry went to 9.30 a.m. Mass, sang with the choir and received Holy Communion. At 6.30 p.m. he attended Evensong. He was now in the bosom of his mother church in Britain.

Henry's friend was introducing him to his friends. They all had jobs and seemed happy. However, on Monday Henry went back to the Labour Exchange to find that the reply to his application had not come. It was now three weeks since he had left the Caribbean and a week since he arrived in England and still he had no work. His wife and children back in the Caribbean depended on him for their financial support. Henry could not wait any longer; he was ready to take any job. He took the initiative and asked whether there were any posts going at Smith's Wire Works at Trafford Park. He was given a card to go to Smith's for a job.

He got a bus and went straight to Trafford Park, saw the Personnel Officer, went for his medical and was asked when he wanted to start work. 'Tomorrow' was his answer. He was given a card and asked to report at 7.30 a.m. the next day. Henry was happy. He went to his friend at work and told him that he had got a job and would start the next day. His pay was £7 per week.

Henry felt a bit strange working among all White men; only one spoke to him the first day. When Henry got home from work he wrote two letters – one to his wife back in the Caribbean and one to his brother and sister in Birmingham. Henry told them how misty and cold it was in Manchester but that he had got a job and was looking forward to meeting the vicar and the nice women in church on Sunday.

When he went to church he was 15 minutes early. The vicar was in the church. He asked Henry if he would like to robe and sing with the choir again. Henry was delighted. He shed a tear when the vicar introduced him to the congregation and prayed for him and his family in the Caribbean. At the end of the service the vicar asked if Henry would like to come to the church hall on Wednesday evening for a meeting.

Henry was pleased to attend the meeting of about eight men. He was asked by the vicar to talk about his life in the Caribbean. Henry ended the talk by giving thanks for all that God had done and for leading him to this parish to join in worship. The vicar then asked if everyone shared the faith and belief in God that Henry had expressed. The reply was almost unanimous: yes they did. Henry noticed that one man did not say a word. The vicar then asked the man to speak. The man got up and said he did not believe there is a God, and he dared anyone to convince him. Henry was so shocked he could not speak for a few minutes. In the Caribbean he had never heard anyone saying that before. He was already experiencing a gap between the picture of a glorified mother church and the reality in England.

On the question of the existence of God, Black people often speak a language that sounds naive and simplistic in the ear of many White English people. In England the existence of God might be an issue to debate, but in the Caribbean Henry had never heard that debate and took God's presence for granted. Black people generally have a deep conviction of the reality of God and there may be a reason for that. Many Black people's experience of God is existential and therefore not debatable. If Black people exist that means God exists. Oppressed groups of people know deep down that God exists, for the sheer reason that they are still here. Psalm 124 illustrates this deep conviction of the oppressed.

> If it had not been the Lord who was on our side – let Israel now say – if it had not been the Lord who was on our side, when our enemies attacked us, then they would have swallowed us up alive. (Ps. 124:1–3)

Many Black people were snatched from their real motherland, Africa, and were taken to the Caribbean as slaves. For hundreds of years they were persecuted at the hands of the slave traders. Yet they have not become extinct. They have lived and have flourished against all odds. In the context of this ancestral history Henry was overcoming obstacles to come to Britain, to find a job and a welcoming church. If somebody had asked, 'How do you know that God exists?' he might have replied, 'All I know is that I was weak and God gave me strength. I was lost and God found me. I was crying and Jesus wiped away the tears from my eyes.' God was to Henry 'a rock in the weary land, a shelter in a mighty storm, and a stronghold in the day of trouble'.[5]

When we go through an experience of wilderness we become more open to God. This is the mystery of God and of our human existence. Many characters in the Bible, but particularly the persecuted African woman Hagar, reveal something of this mystery. In the wilderness Hagar named God, 'You are El-roi', God who sees, and she named her son Ishmael, God who hears (Gen. 16:11–13). This existential knowledge of God is not a debatable issue. Following Hagar's experience many poor and oppressed of the world vouch for the presence of God. They know deep down in their being that God exists. Henry was bringing that deep conviction to Britain. That is why he ends his story by thanking God who gave him the strength and the health to persevere against all odds. God had seen Henry's struggle and listened to his cry and given him strength to persevere. Henry needed no proof of God's presence. No wonder a White person's questioning of God's existence was such a shocking experience for Henry. If it is true that struggling people develop a very intimate relationship with God, this might be a reason why today when Christianity is dying among the privileged groups, it is on the rise among poor and oppressed peoples.

Henry attended service every Sunday for the next few weeks, but he was very lonely. The church people could not really become his family, because their experience was so different from his. Henry's brother and sister and most of his associates were in Birmingham, and Henry was thinking a lot about his family back in the Caribbean. He wrote to his brother and sister in Birmingham that he would like to join them and asked if it was possible to rent some rooms to live together. A week later he got a reply. They found a bigger place and invited Henry to live with them in Birmingham. Henry immediately gave notice at work and told the vicar he was leaving to join his relatives in Birmingham. Church people wished Henry well but were sorry to see him leaving.

Henry arrived in Birmingham on 3 December 1955 and was glad to be reunited with his brother and sister. In the morning he went to the first place he found which was James Booth. A labouring job was offered and he agreed to start the next day. Henry went back home and wrote to his wife. When his sister came in from work she was surprised that Henry had accepted a labouring job. She said, 'You had a supervisory job with the British Government in the West Indies; you should get something better.' Henry told her it was getting near to Christmas and he was thinking of his family back in the Caribbean and he could not be choosy.

Henry was not alone. Peter Fryer claims that most newcomers were settling for a lower job than the one they had in the Caribbean:

> the newcomers found themselves in most cases having to settle for a lower job status than they had enjoyed at home … For, by and large, the jobs they were offered were those the local white people did not want: sweeping the streets, general labouring, night-shift work. In the late 1950s, more than half the male West Indians in London had lower status jobs than their skill and experience fitted them for.[6]

Henry started his new job in Birmingham. The place was noisy, and the work was heavy, but he decided to stick at it and get some money to send to his family for Christmas. He did not work on Saturdays so he went round to inquire of the vicar of the parish. Henry introduced himself to the vicar and showed him the same letter from St Kitts that he had shown to the vicar in Manchester. The vicar in Birmingham was happy to welcome Henry who was such a gifted and active church member in St Kitts. On Sunday the warden welcomed him at the door and during the service the vicar introduced Henry to the congregation. After the service the vicar said that he was a bit short of servers and asked if Henry would like to serve with the vicar at the altar. Henry happily agreed.

There was joy in his heart when Henry told the good news to his brother and sister. The following Sunday he served with the vicar in church. After the service the vicar said he was happy to have Henry's assistance. Some members of the congregation remarked how efficient Henry was.

All went well until the Sunday after Christmas. It was the vicar's practice to consume the remaining bread and wine after communion. He always did this himself, only asking the server to pass the cruet of water. However, on this occasion, the vicar had first to take communion to a woman in the congregation who was not able to come to the communion rail. When he returned to the altar he came over to Henry and handed him the chalice with the wine that the woman had left. Henry reminded the vicar that he had already received communion. The vicar said that he knew that.

Henry took a sip and gave him back the cup. The vicar looked into it, returned it to him and said, 'Drink it all.' Henry reluctantly did. Given no explanation by the vicar, he felt hurt. Why was he being made to drink what the vicar evidently did not wish to drink? Was the woman sick? Was there danger of infection? Was it racism? Black people were often used to doing the jobs that White people did not want to do. This particular incident at communion might have mirrored what was going on in the wider society. A White vicar made a Black server do what he himself did not want to do. Maya Angelou said something to this effect, 'All of us need to be used, but not misused, abused, underused or overused.'[7] That day Henry felt abused. The following Sunday he made sure the service began without him. He went in while they were singing the first hymn. He never served again but still went to church regularly.

After Christmas Henry gave notice at work and looked for something better. He got a better job, but the operator who was responsible for training Henry refused to do so. Someone told Henry that the operator would not train any Black people. The same operator tried in many different ways to cause problems, but Henry persevered. He worked hard and soon became the highest-paid operator on his job. Later he was promoted to become the charge hand.

After two years in the UK Henry had saved enough to send for his wife. In St Kitts his mother looked after the children while Henry's wife joined him in Birmingham and took a job in a hospital. Soon Henry and his wife moved from the area, got better accommodation and started going to a different church. They spoke a lot about their five children back in the Caribbean and felt very sad at times. Henry went to work and asked his supervisor if it was possible for him to work during his annual holiday as he would like to save up to get his children over. The supervisor was delighted. He said during the holiday period he always had problems to cover shifts so Henry could even share in 12-hour shifts if he so desired. From then on Henry was asked to work whenever possible, even doing double shifts if someone did not come to relieve him. Henry worked all the overtime that was available. Some of the men who refused to do overtime were angry when they heard Henry was doing an extra shift. Sometimes when one came to relieve him he would make fun of him saying Henry should really bring his bed along with him. Henry did not mind what they said, his aim was to work and to get the money he needed. It was a struggle but he managed to bring his children over.

His wife and children went to church every Sunday. There was no Sunday school in the church at that time so Henry asked his daughters to get some of their school friends and asked the vicar to start one. The new Sunday school was going well until the vicar's wife asked them to join her once a week to clean church silver and brass. One evening the daughters came in and told Henry that their friends would not clean brass and silver any more, because the vicar's wife did not even allow them to wash their hands when they had finished cleaning, let alone offer them a drink. That was the end of Sunday school. Henry and his wife still saw their children attend church regularly. Their oldest son was a server, but he said the vicar did not seem too keen about him and would prefer not to serve.

One afternoon Henry was outside his house trimming his front hedge. He saw his vicar coming towards him. The vicar noticed Henry cutting the hedge. He crossed the road and walked along the other side. Henry stopped cutting, looked towards the vicar waiting to say 'good afternoon', but the vicar looked in the opposite direction and continued on his way. It is still a common experience for Black people not to be recognised by White church members outside the church. Perhaps White people do not take enough notice of us in the church to recognise us elsewhere. Perhaps we all look the same to them and they can't differentiate between us; or they do not want to recognise us in public. A White woman confesses, 'I noticed about my own racism that I was unwilling to look at people of colour in the eye. I was unwilling to do that because I felt guilty. The effect of that guilt of mine is that people of colour are literally not seen.'[8]

Henry did not let the vicar's attitude deter him and continued to go to church. A few months later Henry's wife went to the Caribbean for a holiday after an operation. Henry took the children to Sunday service. When the service was over, the vicar standing by the door said, 'Mr Brotherson, you look rather pale; what's wrong?' He told the vicar that he had worked last night and had not yet been to bed, as he wanted to accompany the children to church. He also had a busy night at work. The vicar further remarked, 'Look at your hair – you're going grey. If you're working too hard, pack that job in.' Henry reflected: 'Words of consolation from my vicar! I went home with my kids and had a little cry in my bedroom and promised to find another church when my wife came back.'

The White vicar would have thought that he was showing his pastoral concern for Henry and had no idea how he was pushing Henry out of the church. It was not so much about what the vicar did, but what he failed to do. The vicar failed to stand in Henry's shoes.

> Standing in the shoes of another is good, Christian, incarnational theology. It is what we believe God did for us. It is a very revealing way to try to understand what it feels like to be a member of a minority community in Britain today.[9]

Life is still hard for Black people today, but in those days it was even harder for somebody like Henry. The vicar was too keen to speak and advise rather than listen to Henry and understand his situation. It was most insensitive on the vicar's part to advise Henry to pack that job in. He would if he could, but he did not have that luxury.

One day somebody asked Henry how he managed to bring his wife and five children to this country and still was able to run a car. Henry did not give him an answer then, but through his story he wanted to say to him, or anyone else who would like to know: 'I believe in God, and I was blessed with his health and strength for over thirty years' work in this country. My wife trained and worked as a nurse. I had to help with the shopping, cooking and cleaning. I also bake bread and cakes. I do not smoke. I like a drink now and then, but usually buy from the supermarket where it is cheaper. I always wait for the sales to buy clothes and shoes, unless it is something I need urgently. We do not go away every year. We used to save for four years, and then take a short break. Our children are all grown up; our oldest son is residing in Canada. My wife and I are now seniors, still serving God and taking each day as it comes. I know all the problems we Black people have to endure. I do know there are some who dislike us but not all. Let us pray for each other and be thankful to God for all his mercies.'

2
Clinging to the Future

The Reason Why
They left that land of beauty for us.
They left with a friend in whom they could trust:
With God's help they worked hard for their kids; and we
Must not let them down, please try and see.

They never did it for us to drop out of school,
To stand on street corners and act like a fool;
To gwan like we no got no sense in we head
And to follow a path where we might end up dead.

They may not have had much money in life,
They may have worked all hours to cope with strife,
But they showed us a way that was the best of all,
A way to which their forebears had been called.

'Cos when morning come and Jim Reeves licked me ears
And the smell of fry chicken drifted upstairs,
I knew it was Sunday and I had to get up,
To get ready and quickly drink one hot cup.

When I was younger I wanted to stay in me bed,
To listen to music and make it mash up me head;
But there's no arguing in my mother's house –
You went to church or you heard her shout.

But the day I met Christ that's when I knew
Why they had the courage to start anew;
They wanted the best for their kids, you see,
They showed us God; but for their family
They wanted opportunity and a better life,
Education good housing and not so much strife.

You see, but for Jesus I wouldn't be here now,
Coping with life, I don't know how;
No friend has ever been so dear and true
And He's waiting there for all of you;
If you haven't done so to let Him into your life,
His Love has no bounds and reached untold heights.

They came to this country where they met
God's English family who here had been set;
So today we're a nation of all colours and creeds,
But we're brothers and sisters and God is all we need.

So when they send you to church, believe me it's good,
Don't rebel and follow the ways of the hood;
Seek God, try your best, show them nough respect,
It's only then as one nation, we'll achieve success.
AMEN[1]

Janet Johnson

Many Black members of the Church of England share both the experience and the determination of Henry Brotherson. In this chapter two women tell their story. They were interviewed by a younger family member, Simon, who wanted to know more about how life had been for that pioneering generation.

In 1961 Harriet and Hyacinth, two working women, arrived in Birmingham from the Caribbean and began to attend an inner-city church. Harriet told her story. 'Those days I used to walk a long way for the morning service and even for things like midnight mass and Sunday evening service. There were about three of us who walked together. The church was packed with White people. Well, one or two people would speak to you, but many didn't. I used to greet the organist, "good morning", but he would not respond.' Several other people from that church spoke about this organist who had a lot of power. He stayed on in the church until his death and did a great deal of damage for a very long time. He did not like Black people and made it clear by not responding when they asked him anything.

The vicars knew about the organist's dislike of Black people but felt powerless to do anything about it. They were frightened of this formidable organist. That was obvious. In Prayers of Penitence we pray, 'we have sinned against you and against our neighbour through negligence, through weakness …'.[2] Many Christians who are never openly racist are still perpetuating racism through their negligence and weakness. A White woman in the legal profession has come to realise that when she sees racist incidents she feels paralysed:

> I, an otherwise articulate woman who does not often find myself at a loss for words, find myself paralyzed … I am shocked, I am offended, but I don't know what to say. This paralysis is not an accident. I have been taught … 'it's rude to say that someone is doing something bad.'[3]

It is socialisation that often stops Christians from doing what is right in the sight of God. The vicars' inaction let racism continue unabated.

A story told by Martha, who worships in another church in Birmingham, showed how harmful a White person's inaction was for her. In the early 1980s, shortly after she started going to a church, the choirmaster asked Martha to join the choir. He was very nice but when some new people joined, they felt uncomfortable with a Black woman in the choir. Some of them never spoke to her. If she was alone in the choir vestry changing and they walked in, they would ignore her. They used to whisper and when they saw Martha coming they would stop whispering. Martha decided that she was leaving. The choirmaster was fond of her because he really wanted the alto voice. He knew why Martha was leaving but he never said anything to anybody. The choirmaster's weakness helped perpetuate racism in that church.

Harriet knew some Black people from her district back home. They began to attend the same church at 6 o'clock for Evensong. They were told not to come so often so that the church would remain White. Hyacinth added, 'I think at that time a lot of Black people were hurt. They were accustomed to going to church and singing – they had lovely voices. On Sunday afternoon there was nowhere for them to meet up, so they tried to meet each other in church and use their singing voices for God. But after being told to cut down on their visits, they kind of scattered away finding other churches, or even not going to church at all.'

'When you did attend the church', Harriet went on, 'you had to take a back seat – you couldn't go up to the front.' Hyacinth added, once she was sitting on a front seat, and a woman came up to her and said: 'You can't sit there – that's someone else's seat!' This made her feel embarrassed and she got up and went to the back. And from then on, sitting at the back was her position. Hyacinth reflected, 'That's how it was. You had to know your place. White people were trying to tell Black people, "We run this church, you must sit back whilst we get on with it." Black people were afraid of sitting up front in case they would offend someone. Eventually, they got used to sitting at the back. When White people moved away or died, Black people still had it in them to continue to sit at the back. I think that's why it is taking a long time for some Black people to come forward, mingle and do things.' Black people were marginalised in churches and they were physically put on the margins of the church pews. Even today in some inner-city churches it is striking that the remaining few White people still occupy the front seats while in White majority churches Black people go to the back.

Both Harriet and Hyacinth remembered, 'When the service was over, you had to head straight through the door; you couldn't go round for a cup of tea.' For Hyacinth the whole thing was a daunting experience. After coming from a large churchgoing community where everyone mixed together, in this church she felt isolated. She remained an outsider without a chance to get to know who was who and to develop close contacts with people. Years later, one of the churchwardens was the first person to invite Black people round for a cup of tea after the service. Hyacinth reflected, 'It kind of broke the ice. We could mix with the White people and they started to come out of their shell and accept us.'

Before they mixed with Black people some White people had weird ideas. A Black person who worships in another church in Birmingham told us, 'I had a bad experience in the Church of England church I attended. I had my first daughter in 1957. There was an old lady in the church and she thought my daughter was a monkey. She kept touching her – she asked me if she could buy her!' Another person, Ms Yvonne Elizabeth Kelly, talked about her experience in the 1950s: 'It was not unusual for Black people to be looked upon strangely in those days. People were curious and we seemed to be something of a main attraction to them. Ironically while Britain was a great colonial power, to us Black people its citizens seemed ignorant to say the least. I would be asked questions such as, "Where in Africa is Jamaica?", "Do you people have tails?" and "Do you live in trees?" Oftentimes I would be prodded to smile, because the myth was that a Black person's smile offered good luck. In church, no one sat beside me and if by chance I sat beside someone, it was not uncommon for them to change pews. I felt more alone in church than anywhere else.' Another Black person's testimony is recorded in *Church in Black and White* : 'When she presented her baby for Baptism in the early 1950's some White people present lifted the child's robe to see whether it had a tail.'[4]

These incidents say a lot about White people whose humanity was so damaged that they failed to recognise fellow human beings. But how did these Anglicans come to have such damaged humanity? The answer lies in a long history in which European intellectuals created all kinds of racist notions.

> Three notions ... were to be specifically prominent in racist ideology: the idea that Africans were, in one way or another, closely connected with apes; the idea that people with differently coloured skins had different origins; and the idea that human beings could be graded hierarchically on the basis of skin colour.[5]

Peter Fryer shows that 'racism was not confined to a handful of cranks. Virtually every scientist and intellectual in nineteenth century Britain took it for granted that only people with white skin were capable of thinking and governing.' Fryer goes on to say, 'Scientific thought accepted race superiority and inferiority until well into the twentieth century.'[6]

Fryer gives reasons for the creation of racist ideology. It was 'created by the planters and slave merchants out of avarice'. Its function 'was to justify the planters and merchants in their own eyes as well as in the eyes of the rest of the society'. 'It stopped them feeling guilty about what they were doing to their slaves.'[7] Writing in 1984 Fryer asserts that 'Only in the past 30 or 40 years has racism lost intellectual respectability.'[8]

When Black people were coming to Britain in the 1950s and 1960s, racism was just about losing its intellectual respectability. It is a well-known fact that ideas remain alive in people's minds long after they have been discredited. Moreover, these centuries-old ideas do not die naturally; they have to be uprooted by appropriate awareness-building exercises over prolonged periods. Black people can vouch that they do not often see these exercises going on in the churches in Birmingham. But in multicultural areas, through their interactions with Black people, White people begin to understand how to rid their minds of discredited racist ideas.

Because of these interactions multicultural congregations have a chance of becoming racism-free zones, and yet almost all White majority congregations have a slogan, 'We have no racism, we have no Black people here.' One who understands racism knows that the contrary is true. Such congregations are potentially breeding grounds of racism. Their slogan simply shows how unconscious or unwitting racism is in these White congregations. According to the Stephen Lawrence murder enquiry report,

> Unwitting racism can arise because of lack of understanding, ignorance or mistaken beliefs … Often this arises out of uncritical self-understanding … Furthermore such attitudes can thrive in a tightly knit community, so that there can be a collective failure to detect and to outlaw this breed of racism.[9]

It is by knowing 'the other' – people very different from us – that we know ourselves. In tightly knit White communities there is no chance of that. In multicultural churches White people have an opportunity to know Black people and learn about racism, and in that process they begin to know themselves better. Unless White people know themselves, 'Members of so-called privileged groups can seem foolish, ridiculous, infantile, or dangerous …'[10]

Harriet and Hyacinth gave evidence that things improved for both Black and White people only when Black people were invited to stay for tea after the service. Gradually they both began to get involved in various things. Harriet washed the church linen – all the altar cloths; made tea; did the flowers. On a Saturday morning she had to wait outside the church with the flowers for the church-warden to open up for them around 11 o'clock. When the churchwarden came to know how long she had to wait on Saturday mornings he said the best thing he could do was to give her a key, and that's how she came to have a set of church keys. She had an embarrassing laugh when she recalled that in those days she couldn't collect money at public events for the church as she does now. Money had to be in the hands of White people.

Money is power and even today the last thing the Church of England trusts Black people with is money. Here is an example:

> In 1999 the Anglican diocese of Southwark asked the Commission for Racial Equality (CRE) to enquire into its 'institutional racism'… But the facts were that in a diocese with a large number of black people, and some churches with 80–90% black congregations, the proportion of black people attending Diocesan Synod was well below 10%. On bodies like the Board of Finance, the Bishop's Council Advisory Committee and the

Finance and General Purposes Committee representation was nil.[11]

It is scandalous that representation of Black people was nil on two bodies that deal with money: the Board of Finance and the Finance and General Purposes Committee.

Hyacinth remembered that in the 1960s she never saw a Black person taking part in leading the worship service. There might have been a few boys in the choir, but no Black adult had a leadership role. The atmosphere was not friendly. But since she was from an Anglican background she was determined to stick it out. As time went by, new priests came and the atmosphere began to change.

'I would say that the church has come a long way and got a lot better.' Hyacinth continued, 'Is this because there is more of a Black community than the White? I don't know. But there is more friendliness where people work together. However, you still meet a lot of Black people who would not let go of their resentment for the way they were treated. Many decided to form their own church. I'm glad that things are a lot better now, the church is filled with a lot of young people, children, who take part in the service, whereas before you would never see children taking part. Children would have to be seen and not heard. But it's better for the church when children are given a role to play. I think we could do with more Black priests in the diocese to help rebuild Black people's trust and confidence. If only White priests run the churches it seems like a reflection of the old days.'

People like Harriet and Hyacinth paved the way for the next generation. They did so simply by their survival. Drawing on the biblical figure of Hagar, Delores Williams in *Sisters in the Wilderness* shows how survival is a big part of God's redemptive work. The oppressed who believe that God is a liberator of the oppressed often expect instant liberation. Harriet and Hyacinth could not expect that. They took the back seats as they were told. They noticed racism but did not protest. Yet they were deeply involved in a struggle. With their silent defiance they were resisting racism. This defiance was spelt out when Hyacinth said that since she was from an Anglican background she was determined to stick it out.

In many different ways the White congregation made Black people feel unwelcome in the hope that they would leave and the church would remain White. Harriet and Hyacinth survived the unwelcoming atmosphere. They resisted what the White congregation hoped for. This resistance is costly and Delores Williams claims that without God's redemptive power the oppressed cannot survive. Black people in the 1950s and the 1960s wanted the Church of England to become multicoloured and they found the inner strength to remain. This strength was lacking in many White people in the inner-city churches. They retreated and this is why many such churches in Birmingham have now become Black majority Anglican churches.

Simon understands the strength his family members, Harriet and Hyacinth, needed to remain in the Church of England. With many others of their generations they would say, 'I am here to stay; see if you can push me out.' Sometimes Black people born in Britain do not understand the soul power that previous generations had to access to remain in the churches. The young generation is unwilling to tolerate what the previous generation put up with and is often critical of that generation. However, the effectiveness of their sticking power shows that it was a perfectly viable strategy for that generation.

> For everything there is a season, and a time for every matter under heaven … a time to plant, and a time to pluck up what is planted … a time to weep, and a time to laugh; a time to mourn, and a time to dance … a time to keep silence, and a time to speak … (Eccles. 3:1–7)

The older generation planted, wept, mourned and kept silence. The younger generation is plucking, laughing, dancing and speaking out. Had the previous generation not planted there would not have been any plucking for young people today. For young people, time for silence is over; now it is time to speak out. Writing in the African-American context Williams argues:

> The truth of the matter may well be that the Bible gives license for us to have it both ways: God liberates and God does not always liberate all the oppressed. God speaks comforting words to the survival and quality-of-life struggle of many families … But African-American Christian women are apt to declare as Hagar did, 'Thou art a God of seeing' (Gen. 16.15). And seeing means acknowledging and ministering to the survival/quality-of-life needs of African-American women and their children.[12]

Many Black people's stories of the Anglican churches in the 1950s and 1960s are no more than stories of survival. Black Theology too is firstly a theology of survival and then only a theology of liberation. According to James Cone, 'Black Theology is the theology of survival because it seeks to interpret the theological significance of the being of a community whose existence is threatened by the power of non-being.'[13] People are often advised to 'live in the present'. But for oppressed people this may not be good advice. The present is too dreadful for them. They actually have to reject the present and cling to the future. Cone argues:

> Creativity and passion are possible when one stands where the black person stands, one who has vision for the future because the present is unbearable. And the black person will cling to that future as a means of passionately rejecting the present.[14]

Black people look to the past to understand the present, but, since they do not want the humiliating present to continue, a vision leads them to a better future.

When the biblical Hagar went back to the oppressive situation in the house of Abraham and Sarah her present remained unbearable. Yet, she survived because a vision for her future was given to her. In the wilderness the progeny was promised to Hagar, a woman. The angel of the Lord told her that her descendants would be too numerous to count. The God-given future burst into the present and transformed it and Hagar was able to remain in the house of Abraham and Sarah.[15] God's future burst into Black people's lives in the Church of England. They did not collude with the racist situation; they rejected it, yet survived within that awful situation. Instead of simply living in the present they had to transform it by clinging to the future.

Although the struggle has not finished, things have improved in the church for Harriet and Hyacinth's progeny, Simon. A Birmingham-born young man in his twenties, Simon considers himself a third-generation Black British Anglican. His elder family members prepared the way for him and his younger brother. Simon appreciates that his family has a strong religious background. They have lived in the same multicultural area and the whole family has always worshipped in the same church. The church has been a part of his community. His family, church and community made him feel that he belonged in that part of Birmingham. His family has always been very supportive. He has not been unnecessarily pushed but appropriately encouraged by the family.

When he was younger Simon noticed that there was a hierarchy and White people of the 'old school' ran the church. In the PCC (Parochial Church Council) meetings the White ageing middle class made the decisions. There was a gap between the hierarchy and the congregation. Over the last ten years the church has seen a change. White people began to move out. Some did continue to come back to worship, but the church has slowly become a Black majority church.

Simon has always known his family members' stories and been aware of the price they had to pay to remain in the Church of England.

3
Communion! What Communion?

Rejection, Resistance, Resurrection
We answered the call to support our motherland
We were accepted for work, but rejected for worship
Viewed as being emotional, and rather fanatical
Excluded from Religious buildings, though they were half empty

They thought once excluded from religious buildings
Our souls would die of hunger, as we could not worship
They failed to recognise that the church is not the building
But a gathering of God's precious children

This signalled the birth of many black led Churches,
As places of worship we had to establish,
For we needed to fellowship with one another,
They provided a venue, where we could meet together

Some met in bedrooms others gathered in front rooms,
To worship and praise our precious Redeemer
Who protected and guided and gave safe passage
To come to our motherland where our help was needed

In the midst of rejection our faith was made stronger
Knowing God would deliver and give us the victory
We continued steadfast with regular house worship
Until we could rent rooms in community centres

Fifty years later we have built places of worship
Visited by people from many nations
No one is excluded from our places of worship
For we serve a great God who believes in inclusion

We continue to experience a great deal of rejection
And we still have to fight much discrimination
Now we are rejected from gainful employment
But Glory to God we are accepted for worship

We came through rejection and overcame resistance
But through God we triumphed over persecution
Today we are accepted in many places of worship
And many embrace our charismatic worship.[1]

Vilma Jarrett-Harvey

'It was after the Second World War that the Caribbean and Asian people were invited to England to work and live', said Sarai. 'Most of the Black young men had fought in the war, some died, some returned home. Some Caribbean and Asian people came to live in England, Wales, Ireland and Scotland. Some married local people.' As J. Grenville also testifies:

> West Indians, the Blacks from the colonies and the islands had all been welcomed as fighting men during the war, and after 1945 West Indian labour was encouraged to come to Britain to fill jobs for which there were not sufficient whites.[2]

In her early twenties Sarai set sail with great delight to Southampton in England from Kingston in Jamaica. From Southampton she went to Manchester to be with her brother and sister-in-law. England seemed cold and dismal and the houses looked like factories. Sarai began training as a nurse, but saw that a nursing assistant who needed no training earned much more than a trainee nurse. So she gave up the training and worked as a nursing assistant. She earned enough money and since the hours were more flexible Sarai was able to go to evening classes.

In Manchester Sarai first tried a Baptist church, but it was not her scene. She was an Anglican. So she decided to go to an Anglican church. Nobody spoke to her. She knew a few people in Birmingham, particularly George whom she knew well from Jamaica. So in the early 1960s Sarai decided to move to Birmingham. She went to an Anglican church, where the vicar's conversation with her began and ended in 'hello'. It was a church of White people. She sat at the back and felt that nobody wanted her there. After the service she often would walk and look around the church. No one spoke; just blank faces stared at her.

What Sarai said to me mirrored the words of Ms Yvonne Elizabeth Kelly: 'I was indeed a stranger in a strange land. I was not welcomed in the community at large, living accommodation was hard to come by and signs saying, "No blacks, No dogs!" were rampant. Where else but the church does one turn to in times like these when faced with the problems of separation from family, a strange and racist social structure, extreme loneliness, cold weather, and near homelessness? I thought I would have been received more warmly with at least a simple "good morning", however even that was never there.'

Sarai added, 'Sometimes I took the initiative and said, "hello" and "good morning" to people, but they did not have enough courtesy even to return those greetings to me. It was an eye-opener to us Black people to see the so-called educated people who should have known better but they acted in this way.' As already observed, the failure of White people to acknowledge the greetings of their Black sisters and brothers is something many Black people still notice.

Sarai knew that Black people's presence in churches was resented. There was silent hatred written on people's faces. If Sarai tried any seats other than the ones at the back, people had 'Who told you to sit there?' looks on their faces. The church was cold and dark and the congregation made the place even colder. In Jamaica when Sarai was young, Black people were the majority, but there were White English and American children at school. All went to school together. They never treated White people badly. Sarai could not understand why White people treated her in that way. Black people were invited to come to England to live and work. All they wanted was equal respect. Sarai recalled that in those days she could not take communion because there was no feeling of communion in church.

For a while she went to the Methodist church in that area. This was also a White church, and Sarai was the only Black member but people there were friendly. She could enjoy a Sunday service and have a laugh with people who seemed more genuine Christians than the Anglicans. Sarai was asked to arrange flowers. She was invited to the parties and other social gatherings. Communion services were monthly in the Methodist church, but Sarai was able to take communion, because she was in communion with the people. St Paul writes about communion:

> For, to begin with, when you come together as a church, I hear that there are divisions among you; and to some extent I believe it. Indeed, there have to be factions among you, for only so will it become clear who among you are genuine. When you come together, it is not really to eat the Lord's supper ... Whoever,

therefore, eats the bread or drinks the cup of the Lord in an
unworthy manner will be answerable for the body and blood of
the Lord. (1 Cor. 11:18–20, 27)

Racism created division in the Anglican church and Sarai was not
able to take communion with people who were eating the bread and
drinking the cup of the Lord in an unworthy manner. A lack of
racism in the Methodist church proved to her that people there were
genuine Christians and she was able to take communion.

Sarai and George her fiancé wanted to get married, but where?
In the Methodist church which was friendly or in the unfriendly
Anglican church? Both George and Sarai were Anglicans. They had
a lengthy discussion about what to do. After praying and talking to
God they decided to go and see the vicar. When they approached
the vicar, they faced no problem. So they decided to marry in the
Anglican church.

After marriage the couple moved to different areas and went to
various churches. In one parish when the vicar came to visit the
couple he only spoke to George, not to Sarai. Reflecting on this
experience, Sarai described how when you are Black and a woman,
White people's body language tells you, 'You do not exist.' As Sarai
talked, I was reminded of my own painful experience. Many times
by their body language White people have made me feel that I do
not exist. But once there was an extreme case. My husband,
Stephen, is a White clergyman. After our marriage, we lived in
Britain for six years. When I had enough of racism in Britain, we
wanted to go back to the Indian sub-continent. There was a job in
Bangladesh and we decided to live and work there. Sadly, White
racism followed me there.

Stephen was the priest in the Church of Bangladesh for the
so-called expatriate community. This was the church attended by
the British Anglicans – the diplomats, aid workers and others who
were working in Bangladesh in various capacities. These people
often invited Stephen and me to their parties. One evening we were
at such a party given by a diplomat. At that gathering, somehow an
inner circle developed which excluded me. A White English doctor,
a rather quiet and shy person, also found himself excluded from the
inner circle. Standing on the margin of the group we found each
other and engaged in a conversation. After a while the host came to
us and said to the doctor: 'Sorry to have left you all alone here.' I
was shocked: all alone! What about me, was I invisible? The host
managed to insult both of us. The doctor said, 'I am fine here

talking with Mrs Barton', and we remained where we were. The diplomat who could not see me was a member of our church. I was his vicar's wife. We regularly worshipped together. The doctor, on the other hand, was not a member. I had met him only once before as a patient.

During the interviews for this book some people refused to speak about their experience of racism. They would agree with what Ms Yvonne Elizabeth Kelly said, 'There are many stories that I could tell from that period, but some are too painful even to think about.' As I write about my experience the pain and the anger are resurfacing. I know well why some people could not tell their stories. I could not even speak to Stephen about the incident at the diplomat's party for a very long time. When we were invited to similar events I used to have terrible headaches. Those days I took paracetamol tablets and continued to attend such parties. After months of torture I told Stephen about the racist incident and gradually both of us began to avoid parties given by the expatriates.

Sarai knows well that it is double jeopardy when you are Black and a woman. However, she made it clear that not only women, but all Black people suffered a great deal when they first arrived: 'Doors were slammed on our faces, we were denied housing because of our skin colour, we were fighting racism inside and outside the church and we remained integrated human beings. I don't know how that generation of Black people did not become either mass murderers or permanent residents of mental institutions!'

She continued: 'I said I don't know, but perhaps I do know. We survived all these abuses because of the cross. We looked hard on the crucified Christ and understood something of the mystery of our suffering. No affliction could break you when you believed in a God who suffers. We don't need weapons of destruction, we fight with the power of the cross.' When Sarai said this, I thought how biblically based her faith is:

> Therefore take the whole armour of God, that you may be able to withstand in the evil day, and having done all, to stand. Stand therefore, having girded your loins with truth, and having put on the breastplate of righteousness, and having shod your feet with the equipment of the gospel of peace; besides all these, taking the shield of faith, with which you can quench all the flaming darts of the evil one. And take the helmet of salvation, and the sword of the Spirit, which is the word of God.

Pray at all times in the Spirit, with all prayer and supplication. To that end keep alert with all perseverance. (Eph. 6:13–18)

When people in the western Christian world, who have not suffered like Black people, take up weapons of destruction too easily they need to learn from Black people of Sarai's generation. Sarai continued: 'Black people have been treated worse than any other people in the world. In the Bible God is God of the oppressed. That means our God is God of people like us. Without this God on our side we would have faded away, we would have died.' In the 1970s Sarai used to visit patients in hospital. Sometimes even a dying White person would shout out, 'Don't touch me, Black bastard.' If Sarai had been led by her human instinct she would have thumped them. Instead she prayed, 'Lord have mercy on them and forgive them.' She understands that Black people have come to this country for a reason. Many people in this country are spiritually bankrupt; they need Black people here.

Sarai's story went on. Eventually Sarai and her husband came back to the church where they were married. Silent ignoring continued. It felt worse than open abuse, because she was left to wonder what was going through people's minds. Many Black Anglicans were tired of the way White people were behaving and they began leaving Anglican churches and forming congregations in their houses. Sarai and others got together and prayed hard. They prayed for the strength to fight on and for perseverance to stay in the Anglican church. They asked God to send them a good leader. In the 1970s a new vicar came and encouraged young Black people and there was a revival in the church. There was a change in the air: elderly White people dying; other White people moving out; younger Black people filling the vacuum. Some Black people got involved in the church. They became members of the PCC (Parochial Church Council) and Diocesan Synod.

The progress continued in the 1980s. Black members were attending CMS (Church Mission Society) and Christian Aid meetings, which meant visiting different churches and places. Preachers from other churches came to preach. People were getting a bigger picture of the Church of England. Things were better. Sarai's church continued to change. The church that made Sarai feel marginalised in the beginning is now a Black majority Anglican church. But some younger people do not like it when a vicar shows, 'I am in charge,' or talks down to them. People leave, because the church seems cold and dead. Sarai is now comfortable being in a Black majority church, but when she goes to the Diocesan Synod and other committees she feels that there still is this ethos of 'us' and 'them'. She knows that Black people by their persistent presence on these committees give a message that they are as much part of the Church of England as the White people. At committee meetings, although no one would say it, still some White people's body language tells Black people, 'You should not step over the mark. You are here to do the things we want you to do.' Sarai commented: 'It is still difficult to expect much from a church which has treated you as sub-human.'

Sarai is now studying the Diocesan Course for Developing Disciples, generally known as the 3D course. She is doing it for the second time after studying Black Theology. They are studying the Genesis creation stories. During the course she thinks, 'We always learned about the fruit being an apple. I know that the Garden of Eden was not England and the fruit was not an apple.' She knows much that Black Theology has taught her. She is waiting to see whether they are going to be told where the Garden of Eden was.

Sarai has learned in Black Theology that the historic region known as the Fertile Crescent is the biblical world. This is a piece of fertile land surrounded by deserts and seas. The ancient Mesopotamian civilisation grew in this region. If one looks at a description of the Fertile Crescent and then looks at the biblical description of the land watered by the rivers coming out of the Garden of Eden, the two descriptions seem to fit each other. The Fertile Crescent is described below:

> The Fertile Crescent is [a] historic region of the Middle East. A well-watered and fertile area, it arcs across the northern part of the Syrian desert. It is flanked on the West by the Nile and on the East by the Euphrates and Tigris rivers, and includes Lebanon and parts of Israel, Syria, Jordan, and Iraq. From antiquity this region was the site of settlements and the scene of bloody raids and invasions.[3]

According to the biblical description, 'A river flows out of Eden to water the garden, and from there it divides and becomes four branches. The name of the first is Pishon; it is the one that flows around the whole land of Havilah, where there is gold' (Gen. 2:10–11). 'The name of the second river is Gihon; it is the one that flows around the whole land of Cush' (Gen. 2:13). In some versions of the Bible Cush is translated as Ethiopia. The literal meaning of both the Hebrew term Cush and the Greek term Ethiopia is 'black'.

According to Claris J. Martin, 'The word for Ethiopian, "Aethiops", a derivative of the Greek *Aithiops*, was the common generic word denoting a Negroid type in Greco-Roman usage.'[4] The biblical phrase, 'the whole land of Cush' means the land of Black people or Africa. 'In modern times, these two rivers [Gihon and Pishon], following a Latin designation that postdates the biblical text, have been known as the Blue Nile and White Nile.'[5] 'The name of the third river is Tigris, which flows east of Assyria. And the fourth river is the Euphrates' (Gen. 2:14).

According to the description of the Fertile Crescent, the Nile, Tigris and Euphrates are the rivers that watered this fertile piece of land. The Bible seems to be referring to the same rivers, Tigris and Euphrates, Gihon and Pishon (the Blue Nile and White Nile). Coming out of the Garden of Eden these rivers watered the biblical land. The Bible seems to imply that the Fertile Crescent or the biblical land, where Africa and Asia meet, is the place where all life began.

> Recent scientific evidence illustrates that not only are the remains of the most ancient ancestors of man to be found in Africa/Eden, but also the oldest remains of what is called 'modern man' have been discovered not in Europe or China, but in Africa.[6]

> The massive continent Africa was not always known as Africa. This name was given by the ancient Romans. The oldest name of Africa was *Akebu-Lan*, which means 'Mother of Mankind' or 'Garden of Eden'.[7]

Most of the nations mentioned in the Bible are situated in today's Africa and Asia.

Sarai said to me, 'The Bible is our book, not a European book. My birthright was denied when biblical people were portrayed as White Europeans.' She continued: 'When I was younger I was made to believe that in the Bible only Simon of Cyrene was Black and that, like Simon, Black people have to carry the cross.' She has now reclaimed her biblical heritage. Aware that most people in the Bible are Black and Asian, she believes that it is because of racism that attention is drawn to Simon as a Black man. Subjected to forced labour, Simon fits into White people's stereotypical ideas about Black people being slaves and servants. And it is because of unwitting racism that people simply assume that Simon's skin colour was different from that of everyone around him.

This prejudicial presumption is so strong and prevalent that even the publishing house of the Iona Community, which excels at producing materials on social justice, failed to detect its presence right inside a worship resource book produced by them. In order to illustrate Sarai's arguments I am quoting a text from this book which has a Holy Week reflection on Christ on the cross. Simon of Cyrene is one among six biblical characters who speak.

> Simon: I am Simon.
> I come from Cyrene
> And I would not have been in Jerusalem today
> If it had not been for my business.
> I am a traveller.
>
> And perhaps
> I would not have been asked to carry the cross
> If my colour was not so obvious.
>
> 'You ... nigger ... come here!'
> they shouted; and what can a black man say in a
> crowd of white people?[8]

A Black female biblical scholar, Renita J. Weems, knows well how people read contemporary sexism and racism into the texts, believing that they are present in the Bible. She says, 'Indeed one of the earmarks of the current discussion in biblical interpretation is that what one reads out of the texts depends in large part upon what one reads into it.'[9]

In the Holy Week reflection quoted above, European colour prejudice is read into the biblical text. It is assumed that the crowd round Jesus was a group of White people and that the colour of Simon being black was different from the rest. Yet Simon would not have looked any different from many other Jewish people gathered for the Passover from all over the biblical world. It is assumed that forced labour was inflicted on Simon because he was Black, but forced labour was commonly imposed on Jewish people by the Roman government. In Mark 15:21 and Luke 23:26 Simon of Cyrene was coming from the country, in Greek *agros* (field). Most probably he was picked because he was a countryman in the city. Not his colour, but a person's strength would have been a necessary element for carrying a cross. The soldiers would have looked for a strongly built man, rather than a Black man. It is further assumed that the Roman soldiers shared the same colour prejudice as later

Europeans and the use of the abusive anachronistic (seventeenth-century)[10] term 'nigger' only serves to reinforce that impression. In fact many of those soldiers themselves would have been Black Africans.

The impression is given that Simon was a foreigner, but Simon is a well-known Jewish-Christian biblical name. Simon of Cyrene was referred to as the father of Alexander and Rufus, because they were well known in the early church. The Jews and the early Christians included people from Cyrene. Cyrene is mentioned seven times in the New Testament (Matt. 27:32; Mark 15:21; Luke 23:26; Acts 2:10; 6:9; 11:20; 13:1).

Sarai rejects the portrayal of Simon of Cyrene as one Black man in a group of White people. She asks why we still have diocesan courses which do not spell out that most biblical people are Black; they are not White. If the old myths are not corrected in the current diocesan course she is studying, she is ready to challenge. Sarai continued: 'We have been brutalised; our heritage has been denied to us. The church cannot keep us ignorant for ever.'

4
Still I Rise

Still I Rise
Excluded, mocked, yet I stood my ground
Challenging exclusion, cultivated by fear
Prayers mixed with tears as on God I called
Believing that His love would conquer all

Mistrusted, ridiculed, but I stayed calm
Unwavering in my worship and my belief
Enduring suspicion, criticism and pain
Knowing I would triumph in the end

Rejected, persecuted, but still I rise
Soaring like an eagle, to the sky
Not using carnal weapons to defend the cause
But prayer and fasting to the Most High God

'But they that wait upon the Lord shall renew their strength,
They shall mount up with wings as Eagles; They shall run, and not
be weary; and they shall walk, and not faint.' (Isaiah 40:31)[1]

Vilma Jarrett-Harvey

'Still I rise' is the experience of Mr Aubrey Longe. He believes that
much of Black history has never been written and much has been
wiped away. He is one of those people who felt a real urge to record
his story for posterity. Aubrey said, 'Now I believe that a people
without a history is a people that's never existed. A people without
a history is a people lost, so in an endeavour to share with you my
experience of life within the Church of England I need to give you
a background, a synopsis of myself.'

Aubrey arrived in this country in the late 1950s and has resided
in Birmingham ever since. From his childhood he was a member of
the Anglican Church in Georgetown (Blankenburg) in Guyana. He
sang in the choir, served at the altar, polished brass and trimmed

candles. He related that he even developed a technique of snuffing candles with the tips of his finger and not being burnt.

For most Black people of that generation church life was not an optional extra, but an integral part of their being. When Aubrey arrived in Britain, like many others one of the first things he did was to find a church in which to continue in his spiritual development. He found St James, Aston and saw there a large Caribbean congregation in the making and he started going there with his friends. In those days men went to church bedecked in their best suits and women in their lovely dresses and the big hats for which Black women became popularly known. A priest once told Aubrey going to a funeral, 'If you want to find the place, look for the hats, you'll find it.'

After attending St James, Aston for a while, Aubrey found that there was a chaplain for overseas people, the Revd Paul Burrough. Many Black people remember him and think very highly of him. Paul lived in a caravan outside the church and rode a huge motorbike. He befriended Aubrey particularly because his father had served in Georgetown and he wanted Aubrey to meet his father. So Aubrey went with Paul to Oxford and met his father there. Aubrey said, 'I was made very welcome.'

Aubrey was touched by the welcome he received. 'In Birmingham the Bishop had seen the need for a chaplaincy. Paul Burrough was chaplain to overseas people; he looked after their welfare, seeing the newly arrived immigrants of those days settled in. The church was giving a wide range of support not only to us immigrants but also to the host community. People met to introduce themselves and shared cultural experiences. We had Peoples to Peoples Week, an annual event one of which I attended in Witton Road. There was a good lady from Trinidad, Mrs Edwards, who organised and kept that end going. They saw the need for immigrants to be settled in and to be made comfortable.'

When strangers are welcomed, the church touches something of the heart of the Christian faith. In the Old Testament there are more references to helping the stranger than to loving your neighbour. The Bible commands us to love and to do justice to the strangers, the widows and the orphans, the three vulnerable groups in Hebrew society. Verses regarding strangers occupy a huge part of the Bible.[2] The following is one of many such verses:

> God of gods and Lord of lords, the great God, mighty and awesome ... is not partial and takes no bribe, who executes justice

for the orphan and the widow, and who loves the strangers, providing them food and clothing. You shall also love the stranger, for you were strangers in the land of Egypt. You shall fear the Lord your God. (Deut. 10:17–20)

In his teachings Jesus picked up the core themes of the Hebrew Bible. He identified so completely with the stranger that he asked his followers to see him in the face of the stranger (Matt. 25:31–46). In the parable of the Good Samaritan Jesus taught the lawyer to turn strangers into his neighbours by his love (Luke 10:25–37). When Black people say 'I was made welcome', I hear Jesus saying, 'I was a stranger and you welcomed me' (Matt. 25:35).

Once I myself was a stranger in Britain and I could almost hear the heartbeat of people when they told their stories and said, 'I was made welcome.' If people were made welcome at that time, they do not fail to report it today even after so many years. The saying of Kahlil Gibran speaks volumes about Black people's experience: 'The deeper that sorrow carves into your being, the more joy you can contain.'[3] Precisely because we had experienced the pain of rejection carving deep into our being, we were able to contain more joy when we were made welcome.

It is interesting that Aubrey used the stories of the welcoming work initiated by Paul Burrough as a prelude to his experience of rejection. John Wilkinson also writes:

> The intensity of affection with which he [Paul Burrough] is remembered (together with other rare examples of a welcoming attitude or action) shows how exceptional it was. Of the normal experience one example must suffice: 'On my first Sunday in Birmingham my friends and I, we put on our best suits and went to church. But after the service the vicar told us not to come again. His congregation wouldn't like it, he said.'[4]

Aubrey told a similar tale. At Christmas time and on other such occasions newcomers were encouraged to visit the homes of English people. Aubrey liked it and he visited some very nice people in Moseley. They encouraged Aubrey and invited him to attend their church, St Jude, which was then in Station Street, Birmingham. Aubrey went there. Since he had been baptised and confirmed in a church called St Jude in Georgetown, Aubrey thought St Jude would be a place he could go to as well as to St James. So he shared his time between the two churches.

Then one Sunday Aubrey arrived in St Jude when his friends

were not there. After the service he was approached by the vicar and in a very polite fashion the vicar said, 'Um, have I seen you here before?' Aubrey said, 'Yes I've been here before.' Aubrey then mentioned the names of the people he had come with previously. The vicar said, 'Oh, what I want to say to you is this – would it not be in your best interest that you find somewhere else to go?' Aubrey was shocked. He felt bruised. He remembered thinking: 'I came to this country a member of the Anglican Church. Now this young man – my daughter is older than him – is asking me not to come back to this church and saying I must find somewhere else better for me to go. This is the Communion into which I was born, the church my grandparents and my parents took me to. I have come to this country having served with White English priests who were always telling marvellous things about the Church of England!' Sorrow carved deep into his being. Aubrey came away from the church and he told Paul Burrough what had happened. Paul was shocked and horrified.

In the 1950s and 1960s Black people were regularly turned away from Anglican churches in Birmingham. Mrs King told her story: 'The welcome I received was one I will never forget. The congregation was made up of White people. After my second visit the vicar very politely advised me not to come back. He said that there was a lot of unrest and I should give it time to settle. The parish people needed to get used to the idea of having "us coloured people".' Another person was asked, 'Do you know there is a church just round the corner where your people, people of your colour, go?' Black people have been unwelcomed in churches not only in the 1950s and 1960s. Only a few years ago Martha went inside Birmingham Cathedral to hear one of the lunchtime talks. There was a lady standing by the display rack. Martha said 'hello' to her. Instead of answering Martha, she threw down in disgust a book she had in her hand and said, 'Blacks are coming here as well.' Martha got the Provost, and told him what she had said. The Provost searched for her but she had walked out. The Provost said, 'Let's hope she doesn't come back', and then he and Martha prayed for her.

Black people have been unwelcomed in our churches not for what they have done, but for who they are, created in God's own image. Desmond Tutu wrote in a similar context in South Africa where Black people were dehumanised simply because of their skin colour:

Each human being is of intrinsic worth because each human being is created in the image of God. That is an incredible, a staggering assertion about human beings. It might seem to be an innocuous religious truth, until you say it in a situation of injustice and oppression and exploitation. ... To treat a child of God as if he or she was less than this is not just wrong, which it is; it is not just evil, as it often is; not just painful, as it often must be for the victim; it is veritably blasphemous, for it is to spit in the face of God.[5]

When his humanity was assaulted Aubrey understood something of what Desmond Tutu wrote in his own oppressive context: 'It is because God has said this about each of us [that we are created in the image of God] that our faith in God demands the obedience of our whole being in opposing injustice. For not to oppose injustice is to disobey God.'[6] Instead of destroying Aubrey, this potentially dehumanising experience made him a more integrated human being.

Aubrey continued going to St James and thought, 'Well, my long connection with the Anglican Church, my long association with God, the strength that my parents give me, would never allow me to be defeated; so I continued. I saw the church as the basis and strength for my living in this country – I drew on all the resources and resolve that I had and I pressed on. That rejection has strengthened my resolve to fight the good fight on all fronts for justice, racial justice, for involvement in breaking down barriers, opening doors and setting captives free. Recently, the theology of liberation as taught by Dr Mukti Barton has affirmed my ministry.'

Now Aubrey is retired and he believes that there is something deeper in him and that he still needs to give his time for people. He opens doors to claim God for himself and for others. He spoke of his work: 'I must be of the people and for the people so I give my time to serve my community by working voluntarily as an Adviser.' During his work as an Adviser, Aubrey has come to understand that not only White people but also Black people themselves sometimes hold negative views about fellow Black people. 'One day, you know,' Aubrey narrated, 'after I had finished counselling and giving advice, I was asked by one of our own people, "And who are you?" And I was really taken aback – "Who are you?" I had to say who I am.'

It was puzzling for Aubrey when a Black person questioned

him. I think Paulo Freire's reflection sheds light on this pheno-
menon:

> We were in the midst of the campaign for the governorship of
> the State of Sao Paulo, in 1982 ... Lula was the Workers Party
> candidate ... [A] workman ... criticized Lula and his candi-
> dacy. His main argument was that he could never vote for
> somebody just like himself. 'Lula's the same as me,' said the
> workman, with conviction. [7]

Freire understands this as a discourse of self-rejection and rejection
of one's own group. This happens when in a particular society a
group of people are seen as lesser people and are discriminated
against.[8] The above incident of a Black person questioning the
legitimacy of Aubrey's advisory role exposes the truth that in
British society Black people have been made to think of themselves
as lesser people.

Aubrey was puzzled when a Black person questioned him, but
he was equally puzzled when an Irishman who came in to see
Aubrey said, 'I'm glad I'm seeing you.' Aubrey asked, 'Why?' The
man said, 'You're like me.' 'What do you mean by that?' Aubrey
questioned. The Irishman's answer was, 'I'm a paddy and you're a
Black man and we've both been treated the same way. I can open
myself to you, I can open myself to God, the same God for you.' It
was a healing experience for Aubrey and he felt that he was there
for a purpose and doing something worthwhile.

Aubrey expected fellowship from a Black person and experienced alienation, while a White Irishman expressed his solidarity
with Aubrey. Why did this happen? The reason can be found in the
words of Freire: 'As long as the oppressed remain unaware of the
causes of their condition, they fatalistically "accept" their exploitation. Further they are apt to react in a passive and alienated manner
when confronted with the necessity to struggle for their freedom
and self-affirmation.'[9] This condition is known as internalised
oppression, or, in the language of Bob Marley, mental slavery.[10]
Racist conditioning is complete when Black people's souls become
enslaved. They believe the negative portrayal of themselves. People
suffer mental slavery when they remain unaware of the causes of
their condition. When they become conscious they unite with each
other against injustice. The unity among Black and other oppressed
groups is not a given thing; it is a result of this process of becoming
conscious. The Black person Aubrey met was unaware and therefore had no sense of solidarity with Aubrey while the Irishman was

conscious about the oppression Black and Irish people suffer and felt united in the suffering and their struggle for justice.

Aubrey transformed his experience of rejection into resurrection, new life, not only for himself, but also for others. Since that incident of rejection at St Jude Aubrey has held many positions within the church and continued in his ministry in church and society.

'My God is your God, the God of creation. He made me, you and everything that is all around us. For us to survive he has given us the message of salvation through his son Jesus Christ. He died for us, and all of us who were baptised in him and died with him will rise with him.' These words of Aubrey make it clear where he finds the strength to remain in the church and to transform his experience of rejection into resurrection.

The Christ who suffered innocent suffering, died and rose again, is the Christ who has strengthened many Black people from the time of slavery and continues to do so. Black slaves established an intimate relationship between Jesus and themselves. They were sure that Jesus knew what it was to be abused. They sang:

> World treated him so mean
> Treats me mean too.[11]

In their suffering the slaves identified with Jesus to such an extent that they felt that when Jesus suffered and died, he was not alone, they were with him. And in their innocent suffering they were not alone: Jesus was suffering with them. The slaves knew that not Jesus' death, but his resurrection was the last word. God delivered Jesus from his death, which meant that the divine power would liberate the slaves from the death of slavery too. Moreover, Jesus did not remain dead, but was risen and therefore was active in history on their behalf.

Most slaveholders ignored the historical Jesus and used and misused some verses from the Old Testament and St Paul's Epistles in order to keep Black people subjugated. The slaves, on the other hand, drew strength from God's liberating acts in the Old Testament and in the life of the historical Jesus. Kelly Brown Douglas writes: 'It [Christianity] radicalized them [the slaves] to fight for their freedom. This is evidenced by the struggles such as those led by Gabriel Prosser, Denmark Vesey, Nat Turner, Sojourner Truth and Harriet Tubman. These struggles were often supported with Christian themes.'[12]

Confident of their union with Jesus, many slaves felt

empowered to expose the opposition between Christianity and the brutality of slavery, and to resist this great evil.[13] In the same way, today's Black people find solidarity with the risen Christ and expose the contradiction between Christianity and colour prejudice. The Christ who lives in contemporary history energises Black people to resist racism and other ills in society.

Aubrey ended his story by saying, 'I never stay away from the church and from God and I attended St James from that time and I fought the good fight – I fight for justice, I fight for equality. I'm a person, as I told you, who is involved in the struggle to break down barriers. The journey continues.'

5
To Be Free or Not To Be Free

Contemporary Vibes
To be free or not to be free that is the question
Whether it is nobler in the mind to sell your soul
To the trappings of capitalism or to take arms against the sea of
   injustice
And by opposing end them.

To live, to breathe anew, and by that breath,
To commence the movement of a thousand hearts to seek
   emancipation
Tis a consummation devoutly to be wished.

To live, to breathe, to breathe perchance to dream.
Ah but there's the rub
For in that dream of hope only death may ensue.[1]

Janet Johnson

The Revd Canon Eve Pitts came to the Church of England when she
was a young woman. She had a vivid memory of walking into the
local church in an area in Nottingham, which was the equivalent of
Handsworth in Birmingham. People used to think, 'Can anything
good come from this area?' Eve said proudly, 'Yes, I came from
there.' She remembered walking into the local church on a Saturday
morning when she saw a man who said, 'Oh good morning'. Eve
replied, 'Oh good morning to you sir'. He said, 'If you're looking
for the Pentecostal church, it is just down the road there if you turn
left.' Eve's reply was, 'Well, no, actually I'm not looking for the
Pentecostal church at all.' He still did not hear Eve. He said, 'Well
the Pentecostal church is not far, just about ten minutes walk from
here.' Eve was exasperated, 'You obviously didn't hear me, I'm not
looking for the Pentecostal church. I saw that the church was open,
I want a church that's my local church and I'd like to come here.'
   Like Eve I too have the experience of the prejudice that some-

times makes White people 'deaf'. In Southampton my husband was a vicar in a parish and, with our two sons, we lived in a vicarage. One day I was in the front garden talking with our White neighbour over the fence. A White woman was passing and seeing me she said, 'This house used to be a vicarage.' Both our neighbour and I said several times, 'It's still a vicarage.' But she could not hear what we were saying. She went away muttering, 'It used to be a vicarage'. She saw me and could not believe that an Indian woman could have any connection with a vicarage. Her prejudice was so much stronger than the truth that she could not hear it.

In Eve's case the man in the church heard her the second time and knew that she was not looking for the Pentecostal church. She wanted to come to her own parish church. So he said, 'Oh, well I'm not sure you'll like it, it's not your kind of church.' Eve questioned back, 'What sort of church do you think I'd like?' and he said, 'Um well, you people like lively worship don't you?' Eve questioned further, 'Yes, but are you trying to tell me that you're dead here?' He said, 'I'm not exactly certain' in a sort of headmaster voice, 'not exactly but um I don't think you'll be very happy here.' White people often think they know better about our likes and dislikes than we ourselves do. So Eve said, 'Well, let me be the judge of that, what time is your service tomorrow?' and he said, '10.30 a.m.'. 'Fine,' Eve said, 'I'll be here.'

The man had two major wrong assumptions about Black Christians which are as strong today as they were then: first, that Black Christians are Pentecostals; second, that the Anglican Church is a White people's church. Peter Brierley's research shows how wrong the first assumption is. According to his research in 1998 the total number of Black Pentecostals in England was 70,000. After the Pentecostals, the second largest group of Black Christians was 61,000 Roman Catholics, and the third largest group was 58,000 Anglicans. The total number of Black Christians was 269,000. When 70,000 of them were Pentecostals, 199,000 were Black Christians of other denominations.[2] The belief that all, or even the majority, of Black Christians are Pentecostals is no more than a prejudiced assumption.

The second assumption is that the Anglican Church is a White people's church, but the truth is:

> There are now 70 million Anglicans worldwide, most of them in Africa. Though the perception in Britain is of a religious faith

in slow and terminal decline, Anglicanism mushroomed in the twentieth century. And its centre of gravity moved south.[3]

In England itself Black Anglicans doubled in numbers between 1992 and 1998.[4] Looking at the bishops at Lambeth conferences one is convinced that Anglicanism has moved south. Canon Ivor Smith-Cameron asks, 'What are you doing ... to build up your children to live in a world in which the majority of their Christian brothers and sisters will be black?'[5] It seems that most ordinary Anglicans are still unaware of the changes that are taking place in the churches in England and globally.

After speaking to the man in the church on Saturday Eve duly arrived on Sunday. For a long time no one spoke to her, no one smiled at her except one elderly woman who asked Eve where she lived. Eve answered, 'Well I live in the neighbourhood just up the road there.' 'Oh,' she said, 'never seen you before.' Eve knew that for a long time no one saw her in that church. Often White people in the churches claim that they do not see people's colour. Many Black people experience that not only their colour, but they themselves are invisible. The Revd Lorraine Dixon also observed:

> The concept of ethnicity is denied as a lived experience by statements such as, 'I don't see you as Black' or 'I don't see your colour, I just see people' ... How ever this notion of colour blindness is put forward, the result is the same: 'I am not seen!'[6]

It is very interesting to note that Jesus did not have this 'I don't see ethnic difference' syndrome. All through his ministry he made a conscious effort to note the ethnicity of the Samaritans and placed them above the ones from the powerful group. The lawyer must have been absolutely infuriated when in Jesus' parable the priest and the Levite were put aside and the Samaritan man became the ideal for the lawyer to follow (Luke 5:25–37). When others avoided Samaria Jesus deliberately walked through Samaria. He broke down ethnicity, gender and sexuality barriers to recognise the ministry of the Samaritan woman. Jesus' encounter with this woman is one of the longest gospel narratives portraying her as a theologian, preacher and a missionary (John 4:4–44).[7]

The Gospel of Luke deliberately points out that one of the ten lepers who came back to thank Jesus 'was a Samaritan'. Jesus also emphasised the fact that the thankful leper had an ethnic identity different from the rest: 'Was none of them found to return and give praise to God except this foreigner?' (Luke 17:16–17). In such a short story the leper's ethnic identity is positively noted twice. The 'I don't see colour' attitude is contrary to the gospel paradigm. Had Jesus brushed over the ethnic identity of the Samaritans they would have been wiped away from the pages of the Gospels. By naming the Samaritans Jesus both made them visible and left a record of his attitude towards a disadvantaged group in his society. Some White people, by not seeing their ethnicity, make Black people invisible.

For many months Eve was not seen or heard. She said, 'In that church I grew and I died – it was life one minute and death the next. I had to battle against the stereotype that nobody from my area should be articulate and intelligent. No I'm not afraid to say I'm intelligent. Nobody was allowed in my neighbourhood to feel that. It was only during the time of the riots in Nottingham (1958) that I suddenly knew that my church realised that I was a Black person in that neighbourhood, whereas the majority of the people who came to the church were actually from outside. They were White middle class. Now I don't hold it against them except that they behaved as though the local population were just natives and I happened to be one of the natives that they could tame.' Smith-Cameron is also critical of certain attitudes in the church:

> it will be expecting too much if we thought that the second generation blacks would sit down demurely beneath the conspicuous injustice and racial discrimination they see and experience in the life of the Church and often dispensed with such effortless superiority. This seems to be characteristic of the middle-class English – represented so superbly in the life of the C of E, and especially in the clerical and lay hierarchy of the Church.[8]

It was during the Nottingham riots that people really noticed Eve and began to listen to her. It is extremely dangerous for a society when people take notice of the 'other' only when they feel threatened. If a relationship has not been built up between different groups during peacetime, paranoia about the threatening 'other' sets in fast. Since 9 September 2001 this is exactly what has happened regarding the Muslims in Britain. Many British people have become paranoid about the Muslims, because before 9/11 they had not learned to love the Muslims as their neighbours. In Birmingham Diocese people are rushing to study a course on Islam. It is good to do that but if Muslims and Christians are not used to living together peacefully, objective learning about the 'other' during difficult times is hard.

Although during the Nottingham riots people in her church took notice of the Black presence among them, there was little improvement for Eve. She had a tremendous sense of isolation. Her church life felt like a spiritual journey in the wilderness. She was constantly struggling against what people thought she should say and do and how she should behave. During this hard struggle Eve's mother said, 'Well, it's best if you come with me to church. There you won't have that sort of problem.' Eve replied, 'Mum, you've forgotten that when I was younger, they stopped me from going to Sunday school because I asked awkward questions. I can't go back to the Pentecostal church because it would kill me intellectually.' She quickly added, 'It wouldn't nowadays but it would then.'

Eventually her vicar and others in the church realised that Eve was there to stay. She wasn't going to go down the road to the Pentecostal church, for this was her church and she was going to find a place there. So one day when she approached the vicar and said, 'I'd like to be on one of your committees.' He said, 'Oh well um uh well I'm not quite sure whether you ...' Eve could see his hands shaking. She said, 'Well, surely there's a committee that I could be part of.' He said, 'Uh um well we meet at very strange times.' Eve said, 'I'm sure you do, but we could change that couldn't we?' Eventually Eve found herself on the PCC (Parochial Church Council). That was a struggle – again she became invisible in a small group and that invisibility went on.

Eventually, Eve moved from Nottingham to Birmingham. It took her years to learn to cope with rejection, find her voice and claim her true place in the Church of England. She remembered how years ago when she was a young woman she stood in an inner-city church in Birmingham and spoke with some eloquence and confidence. She recalled how she found the language to say that she was one of the young, gifted and Black Anglicans; that the Church of England had to look seriously at its structures. She asked fundamental questions about the church's understanding of resurrection and what it means to be a child of God. She remembered standing in that church and asking, 'What does it mean to be human? And what does it mean to be called church?'

When she went back home, her priest called her and asked if she could come to see him. He said, 'I heard that you've done very well and you're a lovely young girl, uh a lovely young woman, um sometimes um people may be afraid of you because you are outspoken.' 'Well,' Eve asked him, 'are you asking me to shut up?' He said, 'I wouldn't put it quite that way.' Eve pressed on, 'Well that's fundamentally what you're asking me, isn't it?' Eventually they came to an understanding. He recognised that Eve had gifts and as an older priest he had the wisdom to know that it was time for the church to change to accommodate her. He took Eve under his wing and encouraged her gifts. She started to speak publicly in her church and to preach and pray. She began to fly. It was a wonderful time for her.

Eve is one of those rare Black people whose gifts were encouraged by a White clergyperson. Today Eve is a vicar as well as an honorary canon of Birmingham Cathedral. However, many Black people in Birmingham Diocese feel that they had a vocation, but their gifts were not encouraged by their clergy. Martha is one such person. Martha did the Diocesan Lay Foundation Course and then told the rector that she wanted to explore her vocation to a non-stipendiary ordained ministry. The rector asked, 'Have you got a car?' Martha said, 'No'. He said, 'You will need a car. Also it is a very demanding job.'

Time passed and he never said anything more. Then somebody suggested that Martha could go direct to the diocese to talk about her vocation. By this time she was about 50 years old and was told that she was too old for ministry. Waiting made her lose valuable time. She was very disillusioned. Martha decided to do the new lay foundation course called 3D (the Diocesan Course for Developing Disciples). After finishing, she wanted to explore her vocation again, now to the Readers' ministry. The rector said, 'I will see you about that in the autumn.' Seven autumns passed and he never said anything more.

Martha felt rejected by the institutional church, which did not recognise the gifts she was willing to offer. She then had to find out what she could do without institutional recognition. For the last 12 years Martha has been involved in 'Prison Fellowship', which is an ecumenical ministry in prisons. People in the fellowship pray for the prisoners. Martha goes with the prison chaplain to visit the prisoners and to pray with them. Sometimes the prisoners are touched by the prayers and become emotional. Members of this fellowship also befriend lonely prisoners, write to them and sing Christmas carols in prison.

Prayer requests are sent from the prison to the fellowship which meets to pray. For a long period the prayer meetings used to be held in the clergy vestry. Now since the refurbishment of the church Martha can no longer hold the prayer meetings in her church. She said, 'Everything else goes on there, but not my prayer meeting. No one encourages me. I know for sure if I was a White person I would not be disregarded.'

From people's evidence it is obvious that some of the clergy in Birmingham Diocese obstruct Black people's ministry. Indeed, the Church of England as a whole is still failing these people. The Committee for Minority Ethnic Anglican Concerns (CMEAC) produced a report after holding vocations conferences for minority ethnic Anglicans in 1998 and 1999. Ms Smitha Prasadam,[9] Chairman of CMEAC Youth Issues Sub-Committee and Miss Anne-Marie Parker, CMEAC intern, reflected on the conferences. Ms Smitha Prasadam wrote:

> I realized quickly that minority ethnic Anglicans in general and the young people attending the conference in particular were a people of pain. It was evident that those who came needed first to unburden themselves and through individual testimonies there came an outpouring of bottled-up pain from those who ... heard the message: 'Don't send them – they are not good enough.'[10]

Miss Anne-Marie Parker stated:

> what was soon revealed was the sheer variety of talents and gifts they had to offer both the conference and the wider Church. Yet they were all telling us that their resources and skills were being squandered by a Church that could ill afford to waste such abilities.[11]

The statistics support Black people's view that they are not fairly represented among the clergy. In 2004, the total number of clergy in Birmingham Diocese was approximately 372. Including the temporary residents in the UK only about 22, that is 5.9 per cent of the clergy were Black and Asian.[12] According to the 2001 census the Black minority ethnic population made up 29.6 per cent of Birmingham's population.[13] This figure includes many who follow various world faiths, but among those who are Christian there is a higher percentage of churchgoers than would be found in the general White population. Discussing White and other ethnic groups, Peter Brierley's research in 1998 points out that 'in our church congregations there is double the proportion of other ethnic groups as exist generally in the country'.[14] Moreover, many inner-city churches in Birmingham are Black majority Anglican churches where over 90 per cent of the congregations are Black. The number of those churches is constantly on the rise. When these factors are considered it is a serious cause of concern if the White structure continues to bar Black and Asian people from exploring their vocation to ministry. It is urgent that in Birmingham Diocese the percentage of Black and Asian clergy rises above 5.9 per cent.

Mother of three children, Eve has to look seriously at the culture of the church and wonder if the Church of England has changed sufficiently or remains a club for middle-aged White people. Eve continued: 'Well, we do have bright young Black men and women and middle-aged Black women like myself. My young Black son would probably like to be a priest one day – he is highly intelligent, articulate and will be well trained by the time he is about 30. Has the Church of England changed sufficiently for my child to come into it? Or does he have to flounder for six years with a sharp mind before being recognised as bringing something wonderful and creative and liberating to the church? Are you with me? I had to struggle for far too long. I almost left the Church of England.'

Eve talked about a destructive time she had in a church in Birmingham a few years ago. It was a time when she had to dig deep for the strength that God could give her. God did give her strength. Although she had a very hard time, she refused to see herself as a victim. When things went awfully wrong she could have gone on quietly, buried her head and walked away. She could have gone to another church and 'licked her bruises privately'. However, she had no intention of doing that because she knew that unless the church recognised Black presence in a public way it would not get better for other Black women and other Black people in the church. She said that she had lived long enough to hear one of the people who treated her very badly say, 'She is one of the most gifted Black women in the Church of England and we've messed up in a big way.'

Eve did not want to go into any details about what happened to her except to say that there was never a night when she didn't sleep, even with television cameras on her lawn. She received love from people she did not know existed, Black, White, young and old. Some of her own people betrayed her. She went on: 'As Malcolm X put it, and I'm going to put very bluntly, there are those of us who are still quite content to be the "house nigger". I wasn't and I never will be. The song says, "Before I'll be a slave I'll be buried in my grave and go home to my Father and be free."'[15] (Some slaves who worked in the slave master's house, known as 'house niggers', betrayed fellow slaves. Eve used the term 'house nigger' to refer to some of her own people who betrayed her. There is more discussion of the term 'house nigger' in the concluding chapter of the book.)

Since that painful incident Eve has moved on but said she wouldn't forget what happened to her. She deliberately used the words, 'I was bruised, kicked about, raped verbally.' She saw herself as a Black woman who dared to stand up to an institution which has many faults, but is not beyond God's grace and redemption. It is redeemable and is still in process of being redeemed. Many terrible things happened but she found herself a place where her gifts could be used. Eve hopes that the generation of her children and all the young people around will come to find a place not of oppression but of liberation, a place where they can develop.

At the time when she told her story, this remarkable woman had just come back after walking 220 miles on her own to Canterbury. She claimed that many of the people who treated her badly could never do that. That was not just about the physical, but also about the mental, the emotional stamina, the steel. Eve urged: 'We don't need Black people who are boneless today, we need Black people with spine, we need Black people who are willing, Black and Asian, not to simply join the club but to have the courage, the wisdom and the grace to say this is a structure that can be redeemed, a structure which must continue to give life. The institution has good people, good human beings. If it makes proper use of Black people, if Black people are given a chance, they can give the Church of England a bright future.'

6
Refusing To Be Invisible

Untitled
... the journey might be long,
with fire and passion in our hearts,
we know we shall reach our destiny.

One by one we are coming to awareness.
One by one we are committed to a cause.
One by one we are challenging the structures.
One by one we are changing the laws.

Side by side we are bound to make a difference.
Side by side that is how the Spirit thrives.
...
Hand in hand, we can manage any mountain.
Hand in hand we are accomplishing the climbs.

... we foresee the dawn of our vision,
a land filled with honey and milk,
... meanwhile we struggle,
we fight,
we hope.[1]

Kasimbayan

Black is a political term which includes all people who suffer because of their skin colour. In this book this term has been used to include Asian Christians, because they also experience forms of racism similar to what other Black Christians suffer. However, in some ways Asian Christians' experience is distinct. African and Caribbean Christians might be stereotyped as Pentecostals, but Asian Christians are made invisible in British society. To many British, 'Asian Christian' is a contradiction in terms. People generally believe that Asians could have any religion other than Christianity.

In the 1950s and 1960s, in response to labour shortage, people from the Indian subcontinent too came to the UK. In 1957 Mr Talib Masih came from the Punjab in India and stayed in Birmingham for one week. Then he moved to Scotland and lived there till the end of 1958. From there he returned to Birmingham and rented a place in Smethwick from Mr Singh, the secretary of a Sikh gurdwara. Talib never forgot his mother's stern warning, 'Do not ever cease to worship your God,' so one day he asked the Sikh landlord whether he knew of any Anglican church. The landlord told him about St James. When Talib started going to church his first impression was that White Anglicans could not mix with Asian Christians. White people kept themselves to themselves; and being a stranger at that time, Talib did not attempt to mix with people too much. Then the vicar introduced him to the congregation and from then on it became a little bit easier for him. When more Asian Christians came to the area because of Talib they too began to attend St James.

One day in the gurdwara Mr Singh met the Revd Paul Burrough, the diocesan chaplain to overseas people (1959–65), and told him that an Indian Christian was living in his house. Talib, who was visited several times, recalled: 'Once Paul Burrough came with his wife. We had tea and snacks. They also invited me to their place for an English meal. They are really genuine Christians. They both were true friends of the Indian Christians. They looked after us and arranged many coach trips to the seaside and various other places. Indian Christians missed them a lot when they moved away from Birmingham.' When Black and Asian people were desperately looking for genuine Christians, Paul Burrough and his wife were recognised as Christians by their love. At the same time most White people failed to recognise their fellow Black and Asian Christians because they saw no deeper than people's skin colour.

One Asian Anglican expressed his very first impressions of the churches in Britain: 'I went to a White church. Nobody spoke to me. I sat at the back. People did not think I was a Christian. They thought I came to observe the service. Then some of us started a house church for Asian Anglicans. We ourselves led the services. Later on we went to St James Church where after the English service we used to have our service in Punjabi.' Various priests were invited to take the services for this congregation. In 1965 Bishop Wilson, the Bishop of Birmingham, officially welcomed the Asian congregation to worship in St James. Later on the Revd Daniel Chanda, a non-stipendiary clergyman, became the priest for this congregation.

It was not easy to have a service there when people from the previous service were having tea and coffee and talking to each other in the background. If the Asian service was long the White vicar walked up and down showing his impatience. Most probably he wanted to lock up and go home. Mr Jaisher Choudhury reflected that a White vicar's concept of church conflicted with the Asian congregation's concept. Time-keeping was important for the vicar. He wanted to do his job and go home, while for the Asians the sacred and the secular were not separated. They desired the place of worship to be their community space as well.

In spite of some dissatisfaction the Asian congregation continued to worship in St James, but the crucial point came during an Asian Christian couple's engagement in the 1980s. The bridegroom-to-be was travelling from Swindon and there was some trouble on the motorway. He was 25 minutes late. So the then vicar of St James got fed up and asked the Asian congregation to get out. He locked the church and went away. The whole congregation was stranded outside the church. When the man arrived some people went to look for the vicar and they found him in the local pub drinking. The vicar came and took the service. From then on the Asian congregation began to talk about having their own church building. Before very long they had made a decision.

The Revd Daniel Chanda and Mr Peter C. Mall went up and down the country to all Asian Christians of different denominations as well as to the Hindus, Muslims and Sikhs. All these different groups of Asians donated generously towards the church. Women of St James Asian congregation offered their expensive jewellery. The Asians did not go to the English churches. Many churches knew about the fundraising activities but they did not help. The Asian congregation bought an old church from a Black congregation who were moving to a bigger church. A Sikh man put in a bid to buy the premises for storage and was willing to pay more money. But the Black Christians were happy to accept less from the Asian Christians knowing that the building would then remain a church. Within two years the congregation collected enough money to buy the place and renovate it. They named their church 'Good News Asian Church', which was established in 1983. These Asian Christians did not forget to invite their beloved Paul and Mrs Burrough, whose presence at the inaugural service is still remembered with fondness.

Good News Asian congregation gave me this brief history of how their church came to be. One Sunday afternoon they invited me to preach in their church and then to interview people for the book. The interview process was quite different from what I had done elsewhere. The whole congregation, over fifty of them, gathered together to tell their stories. Men and women, young and old sat in groups and were interviewed collectively.

When many African and Caribbean people were resisting racism within the Anglican churches or leaving them altogether, these Asian Anglicans found a halfway solution. They became semi-independent and remained attached to St James. The clergy of St James continue to have a special responsibility for this church. For nearly twenty years Good News Asian Church neither paid into the Common Fund nor did they put their names on the electoral roll. However, now they are beginning to play a fuller part in the institutional life of the parish and diocese.

Open racism, of course, was one major reason why these Asian Anglicans had to find that halfway solution. But they had various other reasons. These Asian Christians played a major role in welcoming Punjabi-, Hindi- and Urdu-speaking Christians from India and Pakistan. Bound by their common languages they were in a strong position to reclaim their common cultural heritage in a foreign land. The exiled Hebrew people cried out: 'How could we sing the Lord's song in a foreign land?' (Ps. 137:4) These Asians were saying, 'How could we sing the Lord's song in a foreign land in a foreign language?' Asian Christians who did not come in large groups had to sing the Lord's song in a foreign language, but these people did not. They found a way to remain rooted in their culture.

These Asian Christians' cultural rooting finds support in the words of the Revd Canon Ivor Smith-Cameron, a prominent Asian Anglican in the UK:

> Christianity by its imperialistic thrust and top-down theological attitudes ... has often had the effect of cutting people off from the roots of their own culture. In China, during the Cultural Revolution, it used sometimes to be said 'One more Christian, one less Chinese!' So at times, in many parts of Asia, Christianity rather than rooting its adherents within their indigenous soil has had the effect of loosening that adherence. Asian Christians are now doing just that, in art, in music, in literature, in liturgy, in spirituality ... We are becoming more and more deeply Christian and deeply Indian: deeply Christian and deeply Japanese; deeply Christian and deeply Chinese.[2]

When Christians from the post-colonial countries come to the UK,

'They are not any longer prepared to allow their history, their roots, their culture to be swallowed up into some pale common denominator – rather they desire their particular gifts to be offered up to God, in a new creative way.'[3]

Mr Peter C. Mall had the vocation to enable Asian congregations to offer to God their particular cultural gifts in a new creative way. He and the Revd Daniel Chanda were the major force behind establishing Good News Asian Church, which is claimed to be the first South Asian church in the world outside the Indian subcontinent. Moreover, for Asian Christians Mr Mall compiled a monumental book which contains more than five hundred hymns in Punjabi, Hindi and Urdu, which are transliterated in Roman script as well. This is the hymnbook that is used in Good News Asian Church and in other Asian congregations such as the Asian Fellowship within the parish of St Peter and St Paul, Aston.

'His [Mr Mall's] passion for gospel music led him to learn a variety of musical instruments, such as sitar, dilruba, violin, harmonium, mouth organ, accordion, piano and the organ.'[4] He was also a good singer. Now his son Mr Amos Peter and others in the congregation use Indian as well as other musical instruments to accompany congregational singing. Through the initiative and encouragement of Mr Mall another church, the Asian Christian Fellowship, came into being in Canada. 'Here Urdu, Punjabi and Hindi speaking people from south of Ontario, Canada and north of the United States gather for worship and fellowship. The first service was held on the 3rd of September 1989 to celebrate the 100th birthday of Sadhu Sunder [sic] Singh, a great saint from India.'[5]

These Asian Christians from the Punjab do not only have their cultural heritage; they also have the heritage of Sadhu Sundar Singh[6] whose day is 19 June in the Anglican almanac. This Punjabi saint, who used to wear the long saffron robe and a turban, never gave up his Asian culture. He was deeply Asian and deeply Christian, and so is the Good News Asian congregation. Mr Mall is the person who greatly inspired this congregation to integrate Christian faith with their culture. The Anglican Church in the UK might not know this man, but World University located in Arizona, the United States, honoured him with the prestigious award of a doctorate in the year 1996. He died in 1998, so for the last two years of his life he was Dr Peter C. Mall.

In many different ways Good News Asian Church is putting forward some of the core values of the Christian faith that are getting lost in many churches in the UK. Here a sense of community is apparent. When many Christian families are failing to stay together, these Asian Christians are remaining strong, whether as nuclear or extended families and as communities. They are there for each other. Theirs is not an individualistic faith; they live and worship as communities of people of several generations.

They have not separated the sacred from the secular. The church building is not only there for a Sunday service. As a community they feel that the building is theirs. They sacrificed a lot to build their own church and they have a strong sense of ownership. Moreover, the social gatherings for all the events of life – baptism, wedding and funeral – take place inside the building. Birthday parties, any thanksgiving events for passing examinations, getting jobs or whatever are brought to God's house. For them God is immanent and there is nothing that is outside God's realm.

In Jesus' life, food played a central part, and in Good News Asian Church food is central. There is a rota for each family to provide the refreshment every Sunday. When there is a special occasion in a family that family usually provides a proper meal for the whole congregation. People from other churches or even other faith communities are invited. The feast is open to anybody who happens to come along. One member smiled when he said, 'We don't have strict numbers; neither do we watch out for the invitees and the gatecrashers. Sometimes you go to an English party and you are asked to pay. This is unthinkable among our Asian community. People just generously give.' Food also breaks down gender barriers in this church. Often men cook and serve the food while women sit down to eat. As in other Black churches, food, hospitality, generosity and service are very much part of the spirituality in this church.

Some Christians in Britain today are leaving Christianity and converting to other religions. I met one such person, a White English Christian woman who has become a Muslim. She explained that she became a Muslim when she was looking for community spirit, hospitality and generosity. She found these not among the Christians, but among the Muslims. I reminded her that these things are not typically Muslim, but non-western and that she would find these qualities among Christians as well. Good News Asian Church is unwrapping Christianity from its western packages and bearing witness to a Christianity which is closer to the gospel.

Asian Christians who are almost invisible in the wider society would have suffered a great sense of isolation without this warm

hospitable church. Here each person's identity is affirmed and celebrated and there is a great sense of belonging. This affirmation of
identity and giving Asian Christians a sense of belonging are the
two most important things that Good News Asian Church is doing.
This church is responding to the danger of invisibility of Asian
Christians in British society. *Don't Call Me Asian*, presented by
Sarfraz Manzoor on BBC Radio 4 on Tuesday 11 January 2005,
proved once more that the Asian Christians are invisible in British
society. Manzoor writes:

> The impact of 9/11 on the US and international security is well
> known. Less noticed has been its impact on Britain's Asian
> communities. Among the first victims of violence after the
> attacks on New York and Washington were not Muslims but
> Sikhs, targeted for their prominent beards and turbans. Hindus
> and Sikhs, frustrated at being mistaken for Muslims, resolved
> to assert their own religious identity. In doing so they were
> sending a message to the rest of the country: we had nothing to
> do with terrorism and riots – that's the work of those trouble-
> making Muslims. For the Muslims, September 11 prompted a
> resurgence of interest in Islam with many choosing to embrace
> their religion as a response to seeing their community vilified
> and demonized.[7]

Manzoor claims that many Asians in Britain now want to ditch their
ethnic identity in favour of a religious identity. They do not intend
to call themselves British Asians. Asians of different religious
groups want to be named British Hindus, British Sikhs and British
Muslims. It is sad if Asians feel compelled to separate themselves
from each other in this way, but all I wish to highlight here is that
nobody is thinking about what we Asian Christians might want to
call ourselves.

These discussions put us outside the Asian communities and
make us completely invisible, as if we did not exist. If we were no
longer to call ourselves Asian, and became known simply as British
Christians, we would be in a bizarre situation, because White
Christians also refuse to affirm our Christian identity. Writing about
post-migration communities, Bhikhu Parekh observes: 'It is true
that maintaining tradition is critical to their self-identities, but their
sense of community owes as much to how they are treated as to
where they come from.'[8] Members of Good News Asian Church
need to belong together as Punjabi Christians, not only because they
come from the Punjab, but also because of the way they are treated

in British society. If they are regarded as non-existent in this society, then it is critical for them to maintain their tradition in ways that affirm all aspects of their identity.

In 1997 Mr Talib Masih had a knee replacement. In the hospital, when he asked a nurse to arrange for him to take communion, the nurse laughed and said, 'You don't take communion, you are a Muslim.' Another person from Good News Asian Church said: 'We hope that people will not always think that we cannot be Christians. More Asians should be encouraged and given a place to become priests and take part in the leading of church services.' Jaisher observed that when he is in his own church he can relax about his Christian identity, but everywhere else it is a constant battle. Recently he went to a revival healing service. Nobody doubted the Christianity of Black and White people, but Jaisher's Christianity was suspect. People were wondering what he was doing there. He deliberately carried a Bible. Even then people thought he was simply curious about Christianity and was studying the Bible.

Mrs Usha Peter, the daughter-in-law of Dr Peter C. Mall, and some other women said: 'People always think that Indians cannot be Christians. We have been Christians for many generations. Our parents, grandparents and great grandparents were Christians. We come from Jalandhar in the Punjab. The English made people think that Christianity is a religion of the English. This is why people do not want to believe that we Asians are Christians.'

The following are some of the things young members of Good News Asian Church said:

✦ 'When people ask me about my religion they are always shocked to hear that I am a Christian. They ask me if my mum or dad is Black or White. When I say, "No they are both Asian," people are confused. So then I leave it at that.'

✦ 'In school I remember people used to say, "How can you be a Christian, you are Indian and what were you before that?" I was born a Christian and my parents were.'

✦ 'People are amazed to hear that Indian Christians exist. Christians from Turkey, Spain and France are really excited to find out that Indians are Christians too. In general there isn't a lot of awareness of Asian Christians in other denominations.'

✦ 'There have been many occasions when I have experienced some sort of discrimination for being an Indian Christian. When somebody asks me what religion I am and I tell them that I am a Christian their response is they think only Black and White people can be Christians.'

+ 'Because people don't believe that I am a Christian I wear a chain with a big cross. Even then people think that this is simply jewellery. If a Black person wears a cross, people have no problem believing that person to be a Christian.'

Good News Asian Church is not only affirming the identity of the Asian Christian members of that particular church, but of all the Asian Christians in Birmingham. One member of Good News Asian Church told me: 'Some people think that we should not call our church Good News Asian Church, but give it a saint's name. They do not understand our predicament. If this church had an ordinary name, when we go in and out of the church the outsiders will think we are people of another faith community who have hired the place. The name Good News Asian Church is constantly challenging people's stereotypes. This name is forcing people to acknowledge our Christian identity.' This church is fighting the battle against invisibility on behalf of Asian Christians who worship in many different White majority churches in Birmingham.

1
The Truth Sets Us Free

What is Truth?
Whatever you conceive truth to be
Just listen for a while and see if you agree with me
You see we've been blinded by thoughts that have allowed
Our past experiences to haunt us and shroud

The fact that we are a people who from biblical times
Have been able to over hardship and troubles climb
Have relied on the strength of our Father above
And we have his seal of approval and unconditional love

The truth is that within all of us there is a spirit of life
That grants us strength and courage to help us fight
Through all the conflicts and challenges that life brings
From which our soul will constantly sing

A song melodious clear and free
Please seek the truth within yourself
And be what you should be.[1]

Janet Johnson

In this chapter I relate and consider the experience of some of the many Asian Anglicans who worship in various churches. They do not have the opportunity that members of Good News Asian Church have of enjoying fellowship and worship in their own languages and culture. However, every day they share the same encounter with others' refusal to acknowledge their Christian identity.

One day I led a service in a chapel in a Christian institution. After the service a White man asked me, 'What religion are you?' He named all the religions except Christianity. Even after I had led a Christian service in a Christian worship place this White man still could not see me as a Christian. The Revd Canon Jemima Prasadam always wears a sari and a clerical collar. People see the sari, but not the collar and ask, 'What religion are you? Are you a Hindu, a Muslim, a Sikh or a Buddhist?' When all the religions have been mentioned she says, 'But you forgot one more religion, Christianity. I am a Christian.' Her daughter the Revd Smitha Prasadam told me about her experience when she was a new student in a Christian college. On leaving worship in the chapel a fellow student asked her, 'So what religion are you?' Another student said, 'I didn't know Asians could be Christians.' A conversation took place between Smitha and a White student:

> WHITE STUDENT: 'When I first saw you, I thought what's she doing here and went and had a big discussion at home. I thought you were just sitting as an observer.'
>
> SMITHA: 'Why did you think that?'
>
> WHITE STUDENT: 'I was convinced you worshipped the elephant God – that you were a Hindu.'
>
> SMITHA: 'Why on earth would you think that? You've seen me take communion, sing in chapel, read the Bible?'
>
> WHITE STUDENT: 'Yeah well. See, you're brown. And in those first few weeks you used to wear an elephant pendant. So in my book you were a Hindu.'

Here is something curious to note: the young Asian man, mentioned in the previous chapter, deliberately wears a chain with a big cross to manifest his Christian identity and the cross is seen as mere jewellery. Smitha wears jewellery with an elephant pendant and she is considered a Hindu. People notice Jemima's sari, but not her clerical collar, because the collar does not fit into people's expectations. They see what they want to see and interpret what they see according to their assumptions.

Hansa Shah was not believed to be a Christian. She told us about her experience. The incident took place in the early 1980s in an inner-city church which Hansa happened to be visiting. There were 'smells and bells' which led her to believe it followed a high church tradition. When the invitation for receiving the communion was extended, Hansa went to the altar along with the others. As she held up her hand to receive the host, a voice from above asked her in a loud and firm voice, 'By the way are you confirmed?' She was quite shocked but managed to reply that she was. Thereafter the elements were duly administered.

For the rest of the service she felt quite unsettled but she told herself that perhaps the priest was particularly scrupulous in performing his duties, perhaps he would see her after the service to apologise for his unwarranted assumption. A few people greeted Hansa after the service, but it became clear that the priest had no intention of coming anywhere near her. She felt that she could not ignore the incident. She sought out the priest, introduced herself and asked him if it was his normal practice to ask every newcomer whether he or she was confirmed before administering communion. 'Oh no,' he replied unperturbed. 'Your people come up here sometimes without understanding what it is all about, just because they see others coming forward!' He seemed entirely oblivious to the hurt and humiliation he had caused her. For what it was worth she told him that if that had been his reason, she would have expected him to see her after the service and apologise for making such an assumption in her case. Hansa does not think she convinced him.

She wondered how often her people, as he put it, really did wander into his church like lost sheep, and imagined that even if they did, he would make quite sure they would not wish to return. For a brief moment Hansa regretted that she was not going to be around in the area to challenge the priest with her presence Sunday after Sunday. She could only pray that over the years he would have grown in understanding about the truth of the gospel which sets all free from the prejudice of gender, caste, colour and race.

The Revd Canon Jemima Prasadam was awarded an MBE in 2004 for her excellent work in the multicultural and multifaith parish of St Paul and St Silas in Lozells. She always describes it as a 'four funerals and a baptism parish'. As so many residents belong to different faith communities, Jemima does not get many funerals, and even fewer baptisms. She is now well known in the area, but still faces stereotypes all the time. 'The incidents that I am going to talk about did not happen years ago,' said Jemima, 'they happened in the last four weeks.' There was a funeral and the undertaker came from a predominantly White area. Jemima opened the door. The young man stared at her. He was lost for words.

I have already mentioned that in Southampton my family and I lived in a vicarage. When I answered the door, people would often ask, 'Do you live here?' I wanted to say, 'No, I just sleep with the vicar,' but I never managed that. A vicarage and an Indian woman seem contradictory to most White people.

The undertaker did not expect Jemima, an Indian woman, to step out as the person who would be taking the funeral. Jemima asked, 'Shall we go?' She shut the door and they started walking and then he said to her, 'Ah, are you to help here today?' She thought to herself, Black people need to have a little bit of wit around them, humour helps. So she said to him, 'Well unfortunately some of us don't get that help – we have to do it ourselves all the time.' He looked at Jemima: 'So you are the person, shall we go then?' They went and sat in the car and then Jemima began to put him at ease because it seemed as if a thunderbolt had struck him. They chatted together, went and did the funeral. And then the undertaker brought Jemima back.

Jemima reflected on the incident. Such events could make Black and Asian people feel rejected, frustrated and angry. Jemima could have thought to herself, 'Look, I am in my gear, I'm in my cassock and everything, and still people can't grasp it. Why should I talk to them?' Instead of retreating into a shell or getting angry with him, Jemima had to find an inner strength to stay calm and remain friendly with the funeral director. 'Black Christians believed that it was God who gave them emotional poise and balance in the midst of oppression.'[2] Jemima accessed her God-given poise and took this incident as an opportunity to break down the man's stereotypical views about Asian women and vicars. She said to herself, 'Let him see what Black people are. They are capable human beings; they can give and receive love and care; they are neither angels nor demons. Let him see.'

Why do Asian Christians have so much difficulty in being recognised as Christians? British colonial history still has a hold on the minds of most British people.

In the 18th century European trade enclaves began to develop on a more systematic colonising basis in the East, and territorial sovereignty was gradually established over substantial parts of India and South-East Asia. At both scholarly and popular levels, a set of stereotyped views of how and why the peoples of the Orient were different and inferior developed. These were based on unbridgeable oppositions between East and West – 'and never the twain shall meet,' as Kipling so infamously put it.[3]

The East and the West became polar opposites. If the westerners were Christians, the polar opposite easterners could be any other religion, but not Christians. The imperial history is the most precious history for White British people, because it gives them a sense of identity; a feeling of superiority in comparison to others. People's minds get stuck in the saying, 'and never the twain shall meet'.

The imperial mind wants to see us as the other, 'the heathen'.

If, by some happy chance, the heathen turn out to be Christians, then they must surely have been converted by westerners. After asking, 'What religion are you?' those people who are time-trapped in their imperial history put the inevitable and predictable question, 'When were you converted?' Since an Asian Christian mind does not bask in the glory of British imperial history, we are free to look at our ancient history as well as at the contemporary world with open eyes. Biblically, historically and statistically Asians are more Christian than the White British.

It is claimed that Christianity was taken to India in AD 52[4] and to Britain more than five hundred years later in AD 597.[5] Recently there has been a lot of scholarly work to reclaim the ancient Indian Christian heritage. Indian Christians have always stated that the apostle St Thomas took Christianity to India in the first century. However, 'the entire historical documentation of the St Thomas Christians was reduced to ashes in the sixteenth century – not by Muslims or Hindus, but by a newly arrived European Christian power: the Portuguese.'[6] It is a miracle that Thomas' tradition has survived this brutality. Indians have kept the marks of Thomas alive in their bodies. These Indian Christian bodies are now the bearers of this convincing evidence:

> Scholars now believe that if the answer to the riddle of the legends of St Thomas lies anywhere it is in [the] rich and largely unstudied Keralan oral tradition.
>
> ...
>
> St Thomas Christians [are] still using the two earliest Christian liturgies in existence: the mass of Addai and Mari, and the liturgy of St James, once used by the early Church of Jerusalem. More remarkable still, these ancient services are still partly sung in Aramaic, the language spoken by Jesus and St Thomas.[7]

For centuries western scholars argued that St Thomas' connection with India was a legend, rather than history. They refused to believe that Christianity could have arrived in 'heathen' India before their own motherlands in Europe. Yet they must have known that Christianity was an Eastern religion. The Bible originated where Africa and Asia meet. India is mentioned in the Bible (Esth. 1:1 and 8:9), but not England, other British islands, France or Germany.

An ancient Christian text known as the *Acts of St Thomas*, dated probably from the early third century, tells the story of St Thomas' journey to India:

At that time we the apostles were all in Jerusalem – Simon called Peter, and Andrew his brother; James the son of Zebedee, and John his brother; Philip and Bartholomew; Thomas, and Matthew the tax-gatherer; James of Alphaeus and Simon the Cananaean; and Judas of James; – and we portioned out the regions of the world, in order that each one of us might go into the region that fell to him, and to the nation to which the Lord sent him. By lot, then, India fell to Judas Thomas, also called Didymus.

According to this book, Thomas did not want to go to India and said, 'How can I, being an Hebrew man, go among the Indians to proclaim the truth?' As he was speaking, a certain merchant came from India, by name Abbanes, sent from the king Gundaphoros. This merchant was looking for a carpenter and Thomas went to India as a carpenter. 'And at dawn of the following day, the apostle having prayed and entreated the Lord, said: I go wherever Thou wishest, O Lord Jesus; Thy will be done. And he went.'[8]

The historical clue in this story was the name Gundaphoros.

> Since AD 1834 numerous coins have been found in the Punjab and Afghanistan bearing his name in Greek on one side and in Pali on the other, and they are dated to be from the first half of the first century ... There is also a stone inscription (now in Lahore museum) containing his name and dates which tell us that he was an Indo-Parthian prince in the north western part of India (from AD 19–45) at the time when St Thomas is supposed to have come there.[9]

The historical date of the Indian ruler Gundaphoros and the date of Thomas' arrival seem to match. It is the middle of the first century. This is not all. Pantaenus, a Christian philosopher sent by Bishop Demetrius of Alexandria, 'to preach Christ to the Brahmins and to the philosophers of India', in AD 190 affirmed the existing St Thomas' tradition in India. Many ancient Christian saints connected St Thomas' name with India. Eusebius (early fourth century), St Ephrem (306–73), St Gregory of Nazianze (324–90), St Ambrose (333–97), St Jerome (342–420), St Gaudentius (Bishop of Brescia, before 427), St Paulinus of Nola (d. 431), St Gregory of Tours (d. 594), St Isidore of Seville in Spain (d. 630), St Bede the Venerable (c. 673–735) and others claimed that St Thomas preached in India for many years and was martyred there.[10]

It is highly likely that Christianity in India is as old as

Christianity itself. Historically India is no less Christian than the UK. Statistically too it can be claimed that India is more Christian in the contemporary world. Data from 1992 shows that only 14.4 per cent of the UK population belonged to a Christian denomination. That means merely 6.7 million people in the UK are Christians.[11] Whereas the total number of Christians in India according to the 1991 census is 19.6 million.[12] In heavily populated India, the percentage of Christians might be minute, only 2.3 per cent of the population, but still the fact remains that today there are more Christians in India than in the UK. The UK is very small compared to India and most people here do not belong to any Christian denomination. The other interesting fact is that Christianity is the third major religion in India after Hinduism and Islam. There are more Christians in India than Sikhs, Buddhists, Jains and others. Indian Christian culture is an ancient culture yet Indians are not considered Christians in Britain.

In Britain, South Asians are also stereotyped as uneducated and uncultured. In the western mind,

> there really is only one culture, and it is both universal and permanent. Within this understanding of culture, one became 'cultured,' and so listened to Bach and Beethoven, read Homer and Dickens and Flaubert, and appreciated Van Dyck, Michelangelo, and Rembrandt. The person of culture, in other words, nourished oneself on the great human achievements of the West.[13]

Anything that is different from western culture is seen as inferior. Moreover, even if an Asian is culturally completely western still that person is not considered cultured. Culture is not biological and we are still judged by our biology, our physical appearance.

Recently Jemima went to buy something in Poundland. The shop was very crowded and she was lost. Eventually she found what she wanted and joined the queue to pay. A young couple were there chatting and having a drink. Jemima did not realise that they were in the queue. When she joined the queue she heard someone say, 'How did she get in the queue?' The couple had taken her to be an uneducated woman who does not understand English or English ways of queuing. Jemima turned around, apologised and said that they could go forward and she would go behind them. At that point the man noticed Jemima's clerical collar. He said, 'Good Lord! You are one of them!' Jemima smiled and said, 'One of who?' Then he pointed to her clerical collar.

Jemima is so used to people's stereotypes about her, she could predict the next assumption. Seeing her clerical collar they would be thinking of her as one from a Free Church Asian Fellowship group of some kind, at least not an Anglican church. In Anglican churches Black and Asian people have heard comments such as, 'Black people are leading! Is this a Baptist church now?' Jemima did not want this couple to make a predictable comment. So she said, 'I am good old C of E (Church of England).' Then the man held her hand and apologised. He said, 'Oh, let's have a hug.' So they had a hug in the middle of the crowded shop. The woman was baffled by it all and a crowd was building up, watching them with some curiosity.

This event had a happy ending, but it is not always so. Sometimes we are like lambs among wolves and all we can do is to wipe the dust off our feet and walk away (Luke 10:3–12). Recently I went to buy something from a market stall. The first thing the shop-keeper asked was, 'Do you speak English?' I said, 'Yes,' but even then she refused to serve me saying, 'Talking to you is like having a hole in my head.' I asked, 'Are you trying to be racist?' She said, 'I can't be racist.' I walked away saying, 'I don't want to buy anything from your shop.'

Hansa Shah was visiting a grand cathedral in the south of the country with a friend. Her White friend was offered an information sheet detailing the history of the cathedral. Hansa was offered none, so she requested one. 'Ah,' said the church guide, 'but in which language? Do you understand English?' 'Adequately enough,' Hansa replied. By this time her friend came up alongside her and chipped in, 'Her English is better than mine.' The guide chuckled, handed Hansa the information sheet and could not refrain from saying, 'Ah, your English must be as good as my German!' In most cases Hansa is able to come up with a timely retort. On this occasion she made none.

On returning home, she thought of the incident and felt that negative stereotypes must be challenged. She could not do much on the occasion but it is her intention to write to the person in charge of cathedral guides describing the incident: about the negative impact these stereotypes can have on those about whom they are made; and the need to educate people who are in positions of responsibility.

We are considered uneducated people, yet in all these three cases we are professional people with graduate and postgraduate degrees. Yet some White people in this country have the audacity to presume that we are uneducated people who do not speak English. We are in fact much more educated than most English people because we can function not only in our mother tongue but also in a foreign language. Moreover, how would it be if English people who visit, live and work in our countries and do not speak our language were considered uneducated?

South Asians such as Indians are usually seen as uneducated people, yet 'university attendance and A-level attainment show that British Indians in particular are matching or outperforming their White counterparts'.[14] Parekh also claims: 'Indians and Chinese are proportionately better qualified than the rest of the population. Nearly 20 per cent of hospital doctors and 12 percent of pharmacists are South Asian, mainly Indian.'[15]

The point here is not to separate the Indians and the Chinese from the rest of the Black and Asian population, but simply to show that a person's religion or level of education cannot be deduced from their appearance. However, Asian Christians often feel pressurised to change their appearance in order to be accepted by White Christians. An Asian woman told us: 'I usually wear western clothes when I go to church, but one day I had my sari on. A White Christian friend surprised me when she said, "Today you are wearing a sari. I thought you were one of us."' Another Asian wrote about his experience when he first became a Christian:

> When I became a follower of Christ, was baptised and became a member of a Baptist church, there was immediate pressure on me to conform. Sometimes directly, often subtly, I was taught how I should now behave and look like a Christian. I did not recognise it then, but see now, the insecurity of my brothers and sisters in Christ who could only relate to me if I re-styled my life to theirs. Not much was relatively said of my life being like that of Christ, who too may have felt the compulsion to conform away from his 'Asian' root.[16]

Asian Christians in Britain find themselves surrounded by many false stereotypes. However, the truth sets us free, because we know that Christianity is very much our religion and we do not have to conform to western ways to prove our Christianity.

8
Stand Up for What Is Right

Sometimes Saying 'I'm sorry' Is not Enough:
A Tribute to Stephen Lawrence

Sometimes saying I am sorry will just not suffice
No, sometimes nothing will pay the price
Of the pain and the hurt that we've endured
And gold and silver is just no reward.

For taking away our dignity and pride you say that you are
    SORRY
For denying us justice and saying, we've lied it's OK 'cause you
    are SORRY
For keeping us down and not educating us you're SORRY, SORRY,
    SORRY
For denying us rights and losing our trust it's OK 'cause you are
    SORRY.

LOOK Stephen Lawrence was yours and mine's brother
So his death has affected every single black mother
When animals are abused uproar and outrage is seen
But his blood cries from the ground and I feel like I could
    SCREAM.

'Cause hooligans can go to France and havoc and rampage cause
And they are imprisoned and Blair apologies to 'nough applause
But for FIVE whole years no apology came our way
And now that it is here what must we black people say?

Hooligans and animal abusers are cast into jail
But FIVE white youths kill and they easily sail
Through the waters of injustice that this country has used
To lock us up and keep us down and us abuse.

So what should we do? Accept the apology?.........Yes
But actions speak louder than words
We must demand that the guilty are punished and stirred
We must write, petition and demonstrate we can't lay back and
    sit
Because we never know who next this oppressor will hit.

But as I've said sometimes an apology is just not enough
But we must not give up there is One whom we can trust
God is not blind and his justice will prevail
No matter what your colour is, through that you'll never sail

So yes we've been knocked down but in the gutter we will not
    lie
We must arise as one and in unity always try
To support our Black brothers and sisters no matter what they
    may face
Whether in Africa, England or America together we can win the
    race

AND PLEASE!!!

Stop taking away our dignity and pride and saying that you are
    SORRY
Stop denying us justice and saying we've lied but it's OK cause
    you are SORRY
Stop keeping us down and not educating us because you are
    NOT SORRY, SORRY
Stop denying us rights because you've lost our trust and we
    know that you're not SORRY!

This poem was written in 1998 when the enquiry into the death
of Stephen Lawrence was launched. During that year after
disturbances in France at the Football World Cup many people
were imprisoned. Also many individuals who had committed
crimes against animals were incarcerated. Stephen Lawrence was
an innocent victim of a racial attack. His story must be
remembered in order that it not be allowed to happen to anyone
again no matter what their colour is.[1]

Janet Johnson

'Recording my personal experiences as a Black person in the Anglican Church is a once in a lifetime chance not to be missed, as to remain silent is tantamount to apathy,' said Mr Tony Kelly. Tony knows the power of the word and is committed to using that power. According to Paulo Freire, 'Thus to speak a word is to transform the world ... Those who have been denied their primordial right to speak their word must first reclaim the right.'[2] Tony has reclaimed that right and believes that this book will be a very significant reference point for future generations to see where we as a people have come from in relationship to the Anglican Church. He acknowledges that it has at times been rather difficult and yet Black people have survived against all the odds. Tony understands that the past, no matter how painful, has a direct bearing on the present and also affects the future.

Starting a sentence by saying 'in my experience' is a powerful way to home in on what it has been like for a particular individual. This is why Tony was keen to speak about his real life experiences – his undeniable reality. However, committing himself to this task filled him with lots of emotions – anger, sadness and happiness – as he had to revisit and recall events and experiences stretching back many years.

As a Black British-born Christian Tony has always been part of the Anglican Church. His Jamaican mother and her two sisters trained as nurses in England and made sure that Tony as a little boy always attended Anglican churches. This was part of their tradition and early upbringing in Jamaica. Tony can distinctly remember that at a very young age as an acolyte in a church in England he was given the task of carrying the incense in its special container for the morning service. From that early age Tony was inspired by the whole ritual that surrounded Christian fellowship and worship.

In the 1960s Tony's mother sent him to Jamaica. He considers his upbringing and education in Jamaica as well rounded and values them a great deal. His education culminated in a teacher's qualification from Mico Teachers' Training College in Kingston. After that he taught English Language and Literature along with Religious Education in three high schools. Alongside his professional life he always played a vital role in the main body of the Anglican church as well as in Sunday school and Youth for Christ conventions.

In 1979 he made an important decision to return to the land of his birth, England, and ever since has worshipped at the same Anglican church in Birmingham. After worshipping with Black congregations in Jamaica Tony experienced an overwhelming culture shock in the church in Birmingham as he saw no other Black people in the congregation. As a hobby Tony sang tenor with the Jamaican Folk Singers led by its founder, the well-renowned ethnomusicologist Dr Olive Lewin. In the Birmingham church the lack of the vibrant, rousing singing of hymns and choruses that he was so accustomed to in the Anglican churches in Jamaica was another culture shock. These experiences left him feeling somewhat alienated, anxious and apprehensive, even though he was welcomed by some of the worshippers. He could easily have moved to a livelier church to worship with more Black people in attendance but Tony firmly believes in the saying that 'a winner never quits and a quitter never wins'. So he stayed. Gradually the music improved with the arrival of a new organist and choirmaster whose more dynamic approach made the choir a joy to listen to and be involved in.

On Tony's return to England his intention was to continue his chosen career as a secondary school teacher. But the local education authority did not recognise his Jamaican teaching qualifications. At that time Tony somewhat naively thought that England would be pleased to have someone with his Caribbean teaching experience. Surely such a secondary school teacher would be better placed to relate to Black students who had an unwarranted reputation as troublesome failures. Tony was told that he could teach only if he was prepared to retrain as a teacher for a further three or four years. At the same time he heard that teachers from Australia, New Zealand and Canada were being allowed to teach after three to six months refresher courses.

The very clear inference was that education in a country run by Black people such as the islands of the Caribbean was not on a par with education in countries run by White people. This is tantamount to racism. Tony's wife, who was also a fully qualified teacher in Jamaica, opted to retrain, but Tony did not. Teaching had always been Tony's first love, yet he refused to abide by this discriminatory practice. Since then Tony has witnessed Britain's education chiefs coming full circle. Now they are regularly recruiting teachers from Jamaica.

Since this book is primarily about church experiences it does not allow space for detailed accounts of all the forms of racism that Tony has experienced in his everyday life and fought against. Yet it is impossible to divorce his church experience from his social and professional life, which impact a great deal on being a Black

Christian in the Anglican Church. Therefore I will briefly outline some of his experiences.

Tony changed direction from his teaching profession and for six years worked as an unqualified residential social worker with teenagers who were in the care of the local authority. But being an ambitious person Tony wanted to become a qualified social worker. He needed his employers to sponsor him. Twice he tried and experienced rejection. Tony thought something was not right and with the help of his union he took his employers to an industrial tribunal under the 1976 Race Relations Act. At the tribunal the all-White interviewing panel members had to disclose their notes which questioned Tony's academic ability, thus revealing the stereotype that Black people lack intelligence. Because of the stance Tony took, a major shift was brought about in that particular organisation's recruitment, selection and promotion policies.

Although he was able to make a difference, Tony resigned from the Social Services department, changed direction and became a probation officer after being sponsored by the Home Office to study full time at the University of Central England. Tony, whose previous employers thought he could not cope with academic studies, gained a Masters degree in socio-legal studies in 1991 at Birmingham University, part sponsored by his current employers. He now works as a middle manager in the equality and diversity unit of the National Probation Service.

Tony gave further examples of everyday racist stereotyping and behaviour. Often when they travel through airports Tony and his family's experience confirms that when a society is racist, no official documents, either a British passport or the proposed national identity card, are a guarantee against racial harassment. The genuineness of these documents would continue to be questioned as so many state officials have yet to grasp that Black British-ness is a reality. Tony spoke about another incident. He came to know that the Chief Officer of the organisation he worked for wanted to know how Tony had managed to afford such a nice home. The implication was that Black people doing well in life are criminals and whatever we have achieved is by ill-gotten gains. Tony could not but complain. About a year later this Chief Officer was dismissed.

As a probation officer Tony has often taken White clients to various places for appointments. Time and again staff at these places would wrongly assume that Tony was the client and that the White offender was the probation officer! Some would then make the excuse that with his surname being Kelly, a typical Irish name, they had assumed the professional was White. Tony gave a particular example. On a visit to a young offenders' institution, a plain-clothes police officer also on a legal visit made a racist assumption. He thought Tony was a family member on a domestic visit visiting an inmate. He took it upon himself to show Tony the door leading to where domestic visits were due to take place. What was so awful about this was that none of the White visiting professionals standing with Tony chose to challenge the White police officer there and then. Tony viewed their apathy as even worse than the police officer's major blunder. Shortly afterwards, one of the assembled group, a visiting psychologist, sought Tony out. She gave him her business card, saying she was so embarrassed at the time and Tony should call on her for support if he planned to take the matter further. Tony told her that her support there and then would have been very powerful and effective. The help was needed then, not later.

Tony did take the matter further. After sending a letter of complaint to the Chief Constable, Tony met the police officer along with another higher-ranking officer at Tony's office. However the police officer still could not comprehend why his helpful action and behaviour, as he thought Tony was lost, was deemed by Tony to be offensive. The police officer further said that he could not be racist as he ran a local youth club which included Black youths. This is the 'I can't be racist, I have Black friends' syndrome.

From the above incidents it is clear that racism hurts Tony almost on a daily basis. People who are hurt by the status quo are the ones who fight to make a difference. Tony challenges racism in his secular life and has been trying to bring about changes in his church in various roles as an altar server, reader of intercessions, lessons reader, member of the Parochial Church Council (PCC) and a member of the Education Committee. When he was on the PCC he was the only Black member, and on occasions Tony felt like a lone voice crying in the wilderness. When White people are the majority a democratic voting process always goes in favour of their ideas. When PCCs fail to take on board fundamental changes that could benefit the growth of the church, the minority Black members are left feeling frustrated. Tony wonders how it would be if sometimes the PCC would hear the minority Black voice and at least have a trial period of implementing the suggestions Black people were making.

The greatest opportunity to make a positive change in the

church came to Tony in 2001. He trained to lead a five-session diocesan course, the *Seeds of Hope: Building A Black, Asian and White Church*,[3] for the members of his congregation with attendance from a neighbouring parish church. This course was specifically designed to increase an awareness and understanding of racism within the Church of England and beyond. For the first time Tony was asking his brothers and sisters in Christ whether they would be willing to face the issue of racism which he has to deal with daily. He was hoping that through studying *Seeds of Hope* together a better understanding between Black and White people would develop. The first session itself was a real eye-opener for Tony. He saw how some Christians he worshipped with on a weekly basis viewed Black and Asian people. These church people had the same stereotypical views that Tony faced in his everyday life.

Two White people were exhibiting racism verbally while at the same time being dismissive of racism, saying it does not exist in the Church of England or among any other Christians. This was mirroring the way the police officer exhibited racism while denying that he could be racist. The apathy in the first session was strikingly obvious, as no one except the other Black participant challenged those White people's racist views. Those two people left after the very first session and only then most of the participants at the subsequent sessions spoke of how appalling the now absent people had behaved. In the secular world the White professionals standing with Tony kept silent when he was being stereotyped by the police officer. The White psychologist came to help not during the incident but afterwards. Both times Tony thought how much more powerful it would have been if White people had had the courage to challenge fellow White people there and then.

Facilitating the first session was a bruising and painful experience. He had to seek out his vicar and me for support. Tony said: 'Sweeping statements, generalisations and negative stereotypes showed how White people perceived us. These had to be heard to be believed. It was an experience that I am never likely to forget.' Tony's experience matched that of Matthew, who said in 1991:

> Basically, what I want is a place that approximates to the Kingdom of God. My understanding of the Fall means that I expect racism six days a week. I challenge it and fight it out there in the world. But in the church there is no mandate, no room for that type of attitude and practice. To be denied as a person and as a people in the very place where you are

supposed to find fulfilment just contradicts the very essence of the gospel as far as I can see. The challenge is the real scandal of racism in the churches – where people are blind to it.[4]

After his painful experience in a group with only one other Black participant, Tony decided to ask a Black university lecturer to co-facilitate the next session. The participants felt that they were being picked upon and had to be reminded that racism is an emotive subject and one is dealing with people's feelings and emotions. Tony always made the point of saying to all White participants that their five sessions of feeling uncomfortable had to be measured alongside the day-to-day experiences of Black and Asian people who have no way of switching off from the pain, hurt and discomfort they endure due to their skin colour. Tony holds the view that if a White person feels guilty at stages on such a course that has to be a good sign. It shows that some movement is taking place. Jean-Paul Sartre also echoes that guilt is a good thing when he writes:

> the only chance of our being saved from shipwreck is the very Christian sentiment of guilt. You can see it's the end; Europe is springing leaks everywhere. What then has happened? It simply is that in the past we made history and now it is being made of us. The ratio of forces has been inverted; decolonization has begun.[5]

About guilt Audre Lorde observes: 'If it [guilt] leads to change then it can be useful, since it is then no longer guilt but the beginning of knowledge.'[6]

As facilitators Tony and the lecturer were constantly challenged by two of the White men but some change in the group was visible. Two White women challenged some of their well-entrenched views. One White man started saying, 'When you come here, we don't want …'. and before he could finish the sentence a White woman interjected saying, 'Don't speak for all of us, with "we".' This was a poignant, powerful and defining moment and spoke volumes at the time. At one session Tony gave an example of racial harassment that he regularly faces in society. Like many Black people he has often been stopped by the police when driving. In the early 1990s Tony was wrongfully accused by two White police officers of a road traffic offence. However, in court, where he represented himself, the three White magistrates found him not guilty. He told the group of another occasion when two police officers

him with his wife and daughter also in the car. When Tony
the reason, he was told that he was driving too slowly. He
iving slowly to get into his drive. But since Tony and his
live in a predominantly White area, the inference was that
nust be from outside the area and up to no good. When Tony
d about this incident, one person in the group asked, 'How can
g stopped by the police be seen as racism when White people
get stopped?'

Writing about comments made at a Christian conference Paul
Grant noted, 'their comments were both politically illiterate and
genteelly racist'.[7] Tony also noticed some of the comments made at
the *Seeds of Hope* course were examples of political illiteracy, genteel
and not so genteel racism. A politically aware person would not ask,
'How can being stopped by the police be seen as racism when White
people also get stopped?' Racism is evident not in the fact that Black
people are stopped by the police, but that in a disproportionately
large number of Black people get stopped.

> Key findings from the 2002/03 research, including the British
> Crime Survey and an analysis of ethnic minority deaths in
> police custody, published on 2 July 04 include:
>> Black people are six times more likely to be searched by
>> police than white people. There are almost twice as many
>> searches of Asian people than white people.[8]

Such research findings are not anything new, but many White
people seem unaware of these realities.

Tony was dumbfounded when a White participant said she
had never seen any racist incident in her lifetime. Tony thought,
'Where has she been living for the past few decades as one only
has to look no further than the media, radio, television and the
press to witness racism manifesting itself before our very eyes
and ears?' Barbara Findlay explains: 'Most White people are
actively socialized first of all not to notice racism, and secondly to
be unable to do anything about racism when we do see it.'[9] A couple of participants spoke of not seeing colour and treating everybody the same. Robert Beckford writes: 'The White superiority complex is a double bind: on the one hand it argues that race does not
matter, while on the other hand, it cultivates whiteness.'[10] In this
climate adopting a colour-blind 'we don't see race' or 'we don't see
colour' approach is the same as cultivating whiteness and denying
a Black person's identity.

Although leading five sessions of the *Seeds of Hope* course was a very costly experience for Tony, at the end of it some people admitted to Tony that some of their deeply rooted views had been challenged, their awareness been raised and they had found the course enlightening. Tony found the courage to run another *Seeds of Hope* course for a cluster of churches elsewhere in the diocese. The all-White participants were far more responsive and receptive to the issues. Tony was encouraged by that positive experience as it helped to restore his faith in human nature. The Church of England, like any other institution in Britain, even with all its Christian values and principles, is steeped in the history of slavery and colonisation and is a microcosm of the wider society. However, Tony wanted the readers to know that it is not all doom and gloom in the Anglican churches in the Birmingham Diocese and that with perseverance and our belief in God we shall and do indeed overcome.

Many of Tony's gifts have been recognised and valued by his parish church and the diocese. In 2001 he was involved in a consultation to find a new diocesan bishop. Two Appointment Secretaries of the Archbishop and the Prime Minister spoke to various people in Birmingham. Tony and other Black and Asian people were able to make a good case for appointing a Black bishop for England's cosmopolitan second city. In Birmingham, Bishop John Sentamu is often spoken of as 'a breath of fresh air'.

The now retired vicar of Tony's parish church was well aware of Tony's commitment, passion and drive regarding equality and social justice and he asked Tony to preach at the family communion service on Racial Justice Sunday (always the second Sunday in September) in 2002. What made his address even more special was the presence in the congregation of one of his aunts who was referred to earlier in this chapter. She was visiting from New York. Afterwards she spoke to Tony of how things had moved on in Britain since the 1950s and 1960s, when the racism she encountered in the Church of England was blatant and overt. In 2003 Tony was invited to engage with nearly thirty new White clergy in the Birmingham Diocese at one of their post-ordination training events (POT) on racism awareness and anti-discriminatory practices. Tony found it stimulating working with clergy with varying levels of consciousness. He hopes that the suggestions and ideas that emanated from the training day are now being incorporated into all aspects of their ministerial life and pastoral care. Tony thought that the diocese should be applauded for organising such training events.

Tony and his wife still worship at the same church some 26 years on. Their daughter has also played her part as a member of the church choir in enriching the beautiful singing. Tony is also pleased to note that the number of Black church members has over the years increased to 12.

Tony's stories are of struggles for justice against racism. People like Tony are often frowned upon by the White churches, but affirmed by verses from the Bible such as the one below:

> Don't underrate yourself. Humility deserves honour and respect, but a low opinion of yourself leads to sin. Do not let others have their way at your expense; do not bring on your own ruin by giving up your rights ... Stand up for what is right, even if it costs your own life; the Lord God will be fighting on your side. (Wisdom of Jesus son of Sirach 4:20–22, 28)[11]

It is when Black people see people's struggles for justice that they recognise the authenticity of their Christianity. In the words of Dr Robert Beckford:

> After all, to be Christian is to struggle against oppression ... Being committed to social justice is about asking questions and taking risks, so that we can alter the structures and systems that oppress us. This is the task of a Black Christian politics of liberation.[12]

Each time Tony stood up for his rights, he had to acknowledge that God was not sleeping and ask the Lord to give him strength to deal with those situations. Tony's belief in Jesus Christ and the power of prayer have given him inner strength to remain focused and firm through all the upheavals, trials and tribulations along the way. Desmond Tutu also understands the gospel of Jesus Christ as 'subversive of all injustice and evil'. According to Tutu, 'Prayer is therefore a dangerous exercise, for it reminds the oppressed of the Christ who identified with the rejected to the point of giving up his life for the liberation of mankind.'[13] Each time justice was done Tony regarded that as a victory for the oppressed over the oppressor. Tony also firmly holds to the view that if civil rights pioneers such as Rosa Parks (who on 1 December 1955 refused to give up her bus seat to a White passenger in Montgomery, Alabama), Dr Martin Luther King and other pioneers such as Mahatma Gandhi, Nelson Mandela, Bishop Desmond Tutu, the Revd Jesse Jackson, Lord David Pitt, Mohammed Ali and many others had not stood up for equality, justice and fair play, a lot of us would not be where we are today. Tony knows that his successes cannot be equated with those people's achievements, but stands firm in the knowledge that often he helped to make real differences in particular organisations by challenging the oppressive status quo.

Tony concludes that he is not expecting anyone to be sympathetic to the ongoing plight of Black and Asian Christians in the Anglican Church. What is required is a degree of empathy, that is, putting oneself in our shoes in order to imagine what it feels like to be constantly on the receiving end of racism. It has an accumulative impact on a person. Tony expects all people regardless of their skin colour to be treated with respect and dignity. He has always tried to embrace, promote and celebrate equality and diversity as an integral part of his everyday life. Even many years after Martin Luther King's 'I have a Dream' speech, Tony remains an optimist. He believes that we can all accomplish the goal of a racism-free society. Racism affects all, both directly and indirectly, and all have a duty to 'Love one another warmly as Christians, and be eager to show respect for one another' (Rom. 12:10).[14] The final thought from Tony is a quote from King's famous 'I have a dream' speech at the Lincoln Memorial, Washington DC, 28 August 1963: 'Injustice anywhere is a threat to justice everywhere.'

9
Paving the Way

African Queens
We are dark, majestic and beautiful and we must remember that,
We have been given by our Creator the wonderful colour Black.
Throughout ages past and present us African Queens have
    grown,
And many a seed of wisdom and love we have sown.
Where shall I start with whom shall I begin?
Let me remind you of the soul sisters that are our kin.
The Queen of Sheba and Cleopatra is where I shall commence
Whose beauty and presence I was told was immense.
Other queens of the Nile have come forth from Africa,
And carried forth messages of joy, peace and wonder,
Harriet Tubman, Mahalia Jackson and Rosa Parkes are others
Who have taken a stand and inspired their sisters and their
    brothers,
Alice Walker, Oprah and of course Maya Angelou
Have shown what self respect and determination can do,
Let me dwell on Maya for a short little while,
To explain why that sister has got such courage and style.
Time and time they knocked her down but like a phoenix she did
    rise
And elegantly brushed herself down and reached for the skies,
Nothing could tame her spirit, nothing would make her lie
Within the depths of despair and cry
So you see
That strong, majestic and beautiful is how they had to be,
And those God-given qualities abide in you and me,
Our Mothers, sisters and grandmothers are all African Queens,
And the ancestral spirit inside us all does teem,
Yes, Africa the Motherland the birth place of us all,
Should always be inside our hearts and we can always call,
Upon our Creator who to us has so much endowed,
Yes, Queens keep your eyes on HIM, and walk tall and straight
    and proud.[1]

Janet Johnson

Mrs Heather Carty is a British-born Black woman who has been an Anglican all her life. Her parents came to England from Jamaica in the 1950s so she considers herself a second-generation Black person in the UK. Heather, a married woman with five children, lives in Birmingham.

She has always worshipped in an inner-city Anglican church that is fast becoming a Black majority church. She insists that she can only speak for herself about what she has encountered and claims that in this church she has never experienced open racism. Heather thinks that in those early years when they first came to England, her parents' generation encountered the harsh reality of racism not only in their everyday lives but also in the Church of England. Through their perseverance and struggle they paved the way for the second generation, so within the church racism has not been blatantly shown towards people like Heather.

Heather told me: 'As a child I attended church with my brothers and sister most Sundays. We went to church in the morning and then would go back in the afternoon for Sunday school and sometimes we would go again to attend Evensong. I never came across racism although I do remember some members of the congregation, who at that time were predominantly White, seemed to look down their noses at us. Was that racism? Or were we being a bit too noisy as children can be? We weren't the only Black children and if I remember correctly a substantial number of the Sunday school children were Black. I would not know how they felt or what their experiences were. I can't say that I never experienced racism because the racism was very subtle in my everyday life, but if I had any in the church then I was oblivious to it.'

As a teenager, like many others, Heather stopped going to church and even afterwards stayed away for several years. Although she left the church, she still had her children baptised there. She felt guilty about using the church to baptise her children and not returning. So after the baptism of her third child she gradually came back to the church and ever since 1989 she has been there. She found the congregation much older and more mellowed and there were more Black members in the congregation. They welcomed her just like an old friend.

She found that her church now had only a small congregation and the Sunday school was not very regular. So one of the things she got involved in was the Sunday school. Gradually she became an integral part of the life of the church and in 1997 she was elected a churchwarden. Neither colour nor gender was an issue since she was the third female Black churchwarden. Heather succeeded a Black woman and her fellow churchwarden was also Black.

As a core member of the church Heather did many things, such as fundraising and visiting unwell and housebound parishioners. She was then asked if she would like to read the lessons in church and lead prayers. Heather felt really nervous about getting up there and reading in front of the whole congregation but also felt privileged to be asked. She was very nervous and knew that her first reading was not brilliant, but was relieved when she was encouraged and asked to continue. In her readings of lessons and prayers she has now grown in confidence. She also administers the chalice and serves when called upon. Although she does not think that she has particular gifts in flower arranging she has even put her name down on the flower rota. She concludes that she would not have been able to do all her work within the church, hold a job and look after her big family if she did not have a very understanding husband who supports her in every way.

Her story in the Church of England is one of success. However, in 2002 she found herself wanting to know more about the characters of the Bible. She felt that she needed to study the Bible in greater detail and read more books. Previously she did not take much notice of Rastafarian preaching about the Bible from a Black perspective, but she had always heard it said that 'Jesus was Black' and that various other characters of the Bible, such as Solomon and the Queen of Sheba, were Black too. In 2002 she really wanted to know more. She knew that if she put her trust in God, then her journey towards the truth would follow.

In 2003 she was very excited when she was able to do a diocesan course in Black and Asian Liberation Theology. Heather said: 'My eyes were opened in such a positive way to see how important Black people were in the Bible and the huge part we played. As a group of people we are so put down and known to our White counterparts as slaves. I had never really studied the Bible as such and only knew the usual popular Bible stories, but what an impact this course had on me. Although I may not have encountered racism within the Anglican Church, the teaching I had been given about the Bible was very deceptive, as God and Jesus were always portrayed as White.'

Heather talked about the version of the Bible she was brought up on. 'As a child at home we had this large Bible. It appeared to be huge to me because as children things are always much bigger. I thought this book was like an enchanting book of fairy tales with its huge hardback cover all embossed and embellished. That's how my memory of it was and we had to be very careful with it and not crinkle or rip the pages. This book was the King James Version of the Bible.'

In many different ways this version, popularly known as the Authorized Version, first published in 1611, has glorified Englishness more than God.

> In the history of the translated Bible, no other translation has achieved what the Authorized Version did by domesticating itself permanently into English life and the English psyche by extending and deepening its hold on English language, character and culture. A. Clutton-Brock wrote that although the Bible came from the East, it had now been 'naturalized in the West, and that the Englishman had fathered what the Jew so long ago begot'.[2] It is amazing to note how a record of beliefs, laws and customs of one particular people has now become a national epic of another.[3]

As the King James Version became a symbol of English nationalism, it became a tool for colonialism.

> [It was] an intruding text that was deeply implicated in the colonizing enterprise. Christopher Anderson ... claimed that the authorised Bible was ... the only version in existence on which the sun never sets ... In the colonies, the Bible as litera-ture, became a disguise for the moral improvement of the natives ... The English vernacular Bible had functioned as more than the Word of God. It had been turned into an icon to make the people obedient to their rulers.[4]

Heather told me: 'Our Bible had colour pictures throughout depicting certain scenes of the Bible and all the characters were White Europeans.' She showed me her childhood Bible, the King James Version reprinted in 1954. This version included 48 colour plates painted by European artists who lived in the years between 1270 and 1675.[5] Heather gives evidence about the damage her child-hood Bible has done to her: 'When I was a child, to me God, Jesus and all people in the Bible were White.'

In this version of the Bible there is even a picture depicting God.[6] God is a bearded White old man who is letting the Holy Spirit descend on Mary. This picture defies biblical commandments, yet it is placed right inside the Bible.[7] In this colonial Bible the invisible God is replaced by a visible White old man. This image says nothing about God, but much about how European theology was putting certain types of human beings at the centre, placing all others on the periphery. A Black British theologian Kate Coleman writes: 'The dominant theology, in its presumptions and assertions, actively displaces us from any position of centrality.' She explains how this displacement has happened: 'I had developed my theological understanding in a context that insisted that the colour of ... God was unimportant unless he was depicted as Black and where God was most definitely Spirit unless *he* was referred to as *she*.' Coleman tells a joke: 'I saw God last night. Really? What's he like? Well, he is a woman and she is black.' She comments on the joke, 'The point being made here is the absurdity of the notion that God could possibly be either.'[8]

With regard to Jesus and other biblical characters, Heather said: 'I knew where Jesus was born but was not really thinking about the type biblical people would have been. I just took it for granted that they were all White. So was I naive? I don't know. Did I just think that whether we are Black, White, Asian, Chinese or whatever, we are all the same and it did not matter that biblical people were depicted as White people? However, these images stayed with me. Now I understand that these White images were like a rejection of Black people. We were dismissed. I knew how Black people have been treated for centuries and portrayed as not worth anything. In Black Theology class the rediscovering of Black people in the Bible made me feel very liberated. Well it was a good feeling – a sort of resurrection for me. That short course has given me a sense of so much pride that I wish all Black people could know the truth.'

But the truth is not easily accessible. Everywhere in the world Jesus and other biblical people have become White.

> Medieval and Renaissance artists, seeking to please those who were in power (and who paid them handsome sums), skilfully employed their oil and watercolors in an effort to reconceive Christianity as a European religion.[9]

The editors of *The Original African Heritage Study Bible* show that the portrayal of Christianity as a European religion did not end with the medieval and Renaissance art.

> In our own time, the revisionist pundits of Hollywood finished off the task. Consider such cinematic 'triumphs' as *The Ten Commandments; The Robe; Ben-Hur;* and *The Greatest Story* (read 'fraudulent portrayal'). Somehow Europeans and European

Americans had magically populated the entire region of Palestine![10]

In 2004 Mel Gibson's *The Passion of the Christ* showed that Hollywood has not finished the task yet. Gibson claimed historical accuracy in the production of his film, yet just about everybody in the film looked like White Europeans. According to *Star Telegram*, 'Gibson's treatment is far more fraudulent than the Hollywood Jesus spectacles like *The Greatest Story Ever Told*.'[11] Both Jesus and Muhammed came from the same region. While nobody ever claims that Muhammed was a European, Jesus has become a White European. As it is wrong to portray biblical people as White, so it is incorrect to depict them as a homogeneous group. 'Ethnic homogeneity has been identified with superiority, connected with the religious concept of purity and used by the authorities to exploit people.'[12]

Anybody with an ounce of historical, geographical, sociological or biblical knowledge knows that the biblical world, situated at a geographical crossroads, could not possibly be the home of a homogeneous group.

> Being in the geographical crossroads between Africa, Asia and Europe, Israel was in the position to play an important role in international trade and commerce. Some of the most important trade routes, between Egypt and Mesopotamia, Syria, and Phoenicia, crossed Israel. Israel offered the only over-land approach to Egypt from the north, and trade routes through Israel were thronged with merchant traffic (Gen. 37.25; I Kings 10.15).[13]

Before the human creation of the Suez Canal in 1869, the whole land of Palestine and Israel was not separated from Africa. The birthplace of Jesus was connected with Egypt in Africa where Jesus as a baby took asylum. When Palestine's proximity to Egypt is highlighted many European scholars try to prove that Egyptians were not Black Africans. However, many biblical and extra-biblical ancient sources prove these scholars wrong: 'Some ancient writers used the colour black to describe Ethiopians. Yet, Egyptians were also considered black-skinned. For example, Herodotus describes the Colchians as "an Egyptian people" because of their black skin and woolly hair.'[14] The biblical people, including the Egyptians, were African-Asiatic people of colour, some of them being African Black. Set in the crossroads of the three continents – Africa, Asia and

Europe – the Bible hardly mentions any places in Europe. 'More of the Bible is set in the region of North-East Africa than in Europe, even Southern Europe; whereas Rome is mentioned about 20 times and Greece 26 times, Ethiopia appears 40 times and Egypt over 700.'[15] Europeans mentioned in the Bible are Mediterranean Europeans.

The idea that the biblical Jews were one homogeneous group is contrary to the biblical truth.

> Now there were devout Jews from every nation under heaven living in Jerusalem ... Parthians, Medes, Elamites, and residents of Mesopotamia, Judea and Cappadocia, Pontus and Asia, Phrygia and Pamphylia, Egypt and the parts of Libya belonging to Cyrene, and visitors from Rome, both Jews and proselytes, Cretans and Arabs – in our own languages we hear them speaking about God's deeds of power. (Acts 2:5, 9–11)

The nations here are mainly Asian and African. The Greek term for nation is ethnos. This shows that the Jews were from different ethnic groups who spoke their own languages. Towards the end of the list two regions in Mediterranean Europe, Rome and Crete, are mentioned. What colour would these Jews have been? Even today many Mediterranean Europeans look more like Asians than North Europeans. Depiction of biblical people as homogeneous White Europeans is nothing but distortion of biblical truth.

Jesus' saying, 'and you will know the truth, and the truth will make you free' (John 8:32) has come true in Heather's life. She has learned the truth about Black people in the Bible and it has made her feel free. Now she wishes this for all Black people. Sadly, it is almost impossible for Black people in the Anglican churches to know the truth. History has put White images of biblical characters in a default position. Unless deliberately challenged by churches, they are going to remain as the accepted norm.

Had White Christianity not made a dangerous liaison with the colonial powers which dominated the world, these White images would not have been as oppressive to Black people as they have become. Some Black biblical scholars write:

> Whites may pretend that color does not matter, because the dominant society as a whole reflects their perspectives and color does not matter to them; but we do not have that luxury ... [T]his history of racial tension illustrates that the real issue goes beyond skin tone: the issue is not color, but power.

> Those with the power want to protect their vested interests ...
> But the powerful do not abuse their power because their skin
> lacks pigment; society's power brokers oppress other people
> because that is what selfish people with power normally do,
> unless they genuinely submit to strong religious, moral or
> social deterrents which would prevent them from doing so.[16]

No human groups can dominate over others without propagating
myths and lies about themselves and other groups. Moreover, the
dominating groups can easily make use of such propaganda
because they control knowledge. The powerful groups usually exalt
and normalise their group by demonising the others.

The great European philosopher David Hume (1711–76) wrote:
'I am apt to suspect the negroes and in general all other species of
men (for there are four or five different kinds) to be naturally
inferior to the whites. There never was a civilized nation of any
other complexion than white.'[17] Another great European philosopher, Immanuel Kant (1724–1804), agreed: 'Humanity is at its
greatest perfection in the race of the whites. The yellow Indians do
have a meagre talent. The Negroes are far below them.'[18] In such a
general climate of racism, Europeans could hardly depict the
biblical civilisation as coming from any naturally inferior, less
perfect human species. Robin DiAngelo writes:

> The demonisation of the one is a prerequisite for the normali-
> sation and exaltation of the other; they cannot be disentangled.
> This identity process is seldom conscious but profound and
> embedded nonetheless ... Privilege serves to reinforce position
> and maintain a state of false consciousness ... This false
> consciousness is the cement that holds oppression in its place,
> and the role of silence and segregation in maintaining false
> consciousness cannot be underestimated.[19]

Anglican churches need only keep silence about the colour of
biblical people and the oppressive status quo will be maintained.
White people will remain in power at the expense of Black people.
However, '"privilege" may confer power, it does not confer moral
strength'.[20] If for their self-esteem, White people have to depend on
untruth, it cannot but be damaging for their identity.

In the last forty years many Black people have become self-
aware and have learned to feel proud of their blackness. When this
self-pride is based on the Bible and God's truth it does not divide
the human race but breaks down the barriers between peoples.

After studying Black Theology Heather said: 'Even though the teachings have made me feel liberated it does not make me feel that we are better than our White counterparts. It shows that whatever our colour, God loves us all, but we Black people have always been made to feel lower than the lowest.'

If White Christians have the humility to hear what Black people in the congregations, Black theologians and Black biblical scholars are saying then perhaps once again both Black and White people will begin to rediscover who they really are, created in God's own image. A White woman realises:

> Those who do not depend on conferred dominance have traits and qualities that may never develop in those who do … underprivileged people of color who are the world's majority have survived their oppression and lived survivors' lives from which the white global minority can and must learn. In some groups, those dominated have actually become strong through *not* having all of these unearned advantages, and this gives them a great deal to teach the others.[21]

Heather understands that as a Christian she cannot hide from the fact that colour plays a part in life. If a person is treated cruelly for being Black, then Heather feels the pain not only because they are Black but also because of the injustice.

'I do feel that the future is good for Black people within the Anglican Church,' Heather concluded. 'We do have a voice and I feel we do get heard. It may have taken a while but all good things come to those who wait. We have to say thank you to our parents who came here and really struggled but persevered and indeed paved the way for us. I have been fortunate in my journey so far to meet people who have encouraged me in my faith journey in the way of the Lord. I am still on that very uplifting journey but am enjoying every minute of it.'

Heather's parents' generation paved the way for her and now in a very significant way she is paving the way for the next generation. Many Black young people of today are rejecting the Christianity that has become a 'White man's religion'. Heather, who is recovering Christianity from this dangerous myth, is well placed as a Sunday school teacher to lead the next generation into the truth.

10
The Proud Black Sheep of the Family

To be Black is Beautiful
To be black is to be beautiful we must remember that.
It is no hypothetical statement but a very true fact,
So never be ashamed of the colour your Creator has given you,
Hold your head up high and be assured that as you do,

The work our Lord has planned for us in this world,
You will inevitably face opposition and abuse they may hurl.
Into your path to plant seeds of insecurity and doubt,
But you can rest assured that God will help you to mount,
Above the jangling discords that in your path are thrown,
And it won't be long before you have grown

Strong, black and beautiful and more precious in His sight,
Any prejudice and inequality He will help you to fight,
Not by violence or other demeaning means,
But with prayer wisdom and perseverance the climb ahead will
    seem
Possible, achievable, and we know we must keep on,
Fighting for future generations until they have won,
The respect and rights that to them are due,
The very rights that have been denied from me and you.

We must teach them black is beautiful no matter what anyone
    may say
My friends keep this thought in your minds each and every day.
AMEN[1]

Janet Johnson

'"Nigger!" screamed Trevor, as I walked away from our argument.
That word stopped me in my tracks. I dropped my prized red
Raleigh Grifter Bike and ran back towards him – to give him a few
thumps! I wanted to hurt him as much as he hurt me. We were both

eleven. My brother Michael and best friend Lorraine had been watching the argument escalate and heard the remark. Being Black themselves, as well as from the look on my face, both knew what was about to happen. They both ran to stop me. A few more steps and I would be there. Then I heard Lorraine scream "No Jacquie!" With my clenched fist fast approaching him, Trevor looked petrified. Fortunately or unfortunately they got to me before I got Trevor. Lucky for him.'

Jacquie vividly remembered the pain of being called 'nigger' when she was 11 years old. Trevor was the son of their neighbour. They had grown up together, played games of darts and chess. They were friends. Trevor was a haemophiliac and had been given strict instructions not to ride Jacquie's bike, in case he fell off and cut himself. Being a haemophiliac a simple cut would result in hours of tests and doses of factor 8 in casualty. However, being 11 he decided he would take Jacquie's bike without her permission and ride like the wind. When she caught the back of the seat and stopped him, all for his own good, this is how he repaid Jacquie.

Since then the word 'nigger' has sent feelings of hatred, resentment and anger flowing through Jacquie's veins on many occasions. The word actually used to hit her so hard she felt winded and breathless, lost for words too. She used to think, 'What could be an apt reply to such an insult, other than a slap or thump?'

'Words are wind but blows are unkind' is a saying Jacquie's mother used to soothe her as a child (and adult) when she had been upset. Jacquie was not convinced. She knew blows are unkind and words can wound too. Sometimes words wound more deeply than any blow. Racist terms hurt a great deal. For example the word 'nigger', the literal meaning of which is black, is much more than a word, because it is connected with the history of colonialism and slavery. 'The English colonialists and slave entity borrowed the term "Negro" from the Spanish … The English slave owners degraded and defiled the … name by turning the Negro into a slave.'[2] Strong anger in Black people is generated by this term, because it is connected with the painful memory of the long history of racist oppression.

As a young girl Jacquie had to carry this painful history and work out how to transform her feelings of hurt and anger, and work towards creating a better environment in Lea Mason Church of England Secondary School. The students were from all backgrounds and cultures. Jacquie and a group of friends formed a little cluster of individuals. The common denominator for this group of

Black, White and Asian students was that they were sick and tired of racism and other kinds of colour or sex oppression. The group was called the 'Benetton Posse' (based on the Benetton Clothing Company who are infamous for running hard-hitting advertising campaigns featuring women and men from all cultures, colours and nationalities). They never did get to count how many members were involved, but there were at least twenty to thirty regular individuals. As a 'posse' the group stuck to the principle that 'All are Equal' and policed the school grounds identifying any fights or arguments based on racism. When they did expose such things, members would intervene and report back to the teachers.

The Benetton Posse philosophy has followed Jacquie throughout her adult life. The principles of 'All are Equal' have been and are still Jacquie's guide – her 'Internal Compass'. She knows that young people have heard stories from their grandparents and parents of being scorned when they arrived in this country. Signs in guesthouses read, 'No Dogs, No Irish, No Coloured (Niggers, Pakis or Darkies)'. She reads tabloid headlines about Black-on-Black violence and reports of Black youths being labelled as drug dealers because they were standing around in their local shopping precinct. Even if they went to the shop to buy a loaf of bread for their mother and stopped to say hello to a school friend before going home, they would be accused of selling drugs. Some Asians are stereotyped as taxi drivers or terrorists. Jacquie is not surprised that there are so many atrocities happening all over the world, because oppressed people are getting angry and 'sick and tired of being sick and tired!' Church is a place that people enter to find rest and refuge. But when Jacquie, wearied by racism, goes to church she finds it there too. Only, in the church, racism is often masked by the slogan 'We treat all people the same'.

I am a gardener and I know that I cannot treat all the plants in the same way. If I plant perpetual spinach and aubergines in the garden, the spinach will flourish and the aubergines will bear no fruit. The aubergines need to be put into the greenhouse. When churches say 'We treat Black and White people in the same way', it is the same as saying, 'We will let White people flourish and we do not care if the same treatment is not good enough for Black people.'

Churches need to find out in what ways they are failing Black people. Jacquie says, 'I love communication in listening, reading, writing and talking. I love to see people communicate in the ways most apt. During church services I listen not only to what is being said, but also what words/terminology are used. During PCC

(Parochial Church Council) and general conversation I hear the word black used in a negative fashion. "Oh don't blacken the atmosphere. It's not all black! There is good news." These comments hurt.'

Black people feel hurt that church members who use such expressions are usually completely unaware that by their use of language they keep racism intact. An article in the *Saturday Review* reads:

> People in Western cultures do not realize the extent to which their racial attitudes have been conditioned since early childhood by the power of words to ennoble or condemn, augment or detract, glorify or demean. Negative language infects the subconscious of most Western people from the time they first learn to speak. Prejudice is not merely imparted or superimposed. It is metabolized in the bloodstream of society.[3]

If colour prejudicial language is metabolised in the bloodstream of society and therefore in church, church people need to be aware of it. Awareness or consciousness makes us realise how conditioned we are. This awareness can come from listening to a conscious Black woman like Jacquie. However, churchgoers generally are not very good at listening to Black people. David Haslam, a White clergyman speaks from his experience:

> The first important step is to *listen* to what people from black and minority communities say. It is extraordinary how white people always think they know better, even than those whose experience is being discussed. Like Job's friends, white people need to sit and listen, feel the pain, and sometimes wait for quite a long time before black people are prepared to tell them how they really feel.[4]

When we are able to listen, we become conscious. Genuine consciousness always has an effect on us. Robert Moore writes: 'While we may not be able to change the language, we can definitely change our usage of the language. We can avoid using words that degrade people.'[5] I take Moore's argument further by saying, maybe not overnight, but we can change a language. A living language is bound to change. We as church people can begin the process of that positive change in the English language.

However, when Black people urge church members to avoid using words that are harmful for their Black identity, they are told that this is secular political correctness – as if to say church people do not have to use politically correct language since it originated in secular society. A dictionary meaning of political correctness is: 'the avoidance of forms of expression or action that are perceived to exclude, marginalize, or insult groups of people who are socially disadvantaged or discriminated against'.[6] Church people who are supposed to be guided by the principle of loving one's neighbour as oneself should not really have any problem with the principle of political correctness.

One could even argue that Jesus in his own time introduced politically correct language. An example is found in Luke 13:16. The Bible gives long lists of sons of Abraham and forgets the daughters. Jesus redresses the balance. He refers to the bent woman in Luke as a daughter of Abraham. In fact this is the only time in the whole Bible that a woman is given this title. Jesus, a man, was able to stand in the shoes of a woman to understand how it felt for a woman never to be given the title of daughter of Abraham. Jesus redressed the balance by using inclusive language. Language does have power. Jesus harnessed that power in favour of women who were socially disadvantaged or discriminated against, women who felt excluded, marginalised, or insulted by forms of expression.[7] When we are able to stand in the shoes of another, we would never use words or phrases that hurt or marginalise their people.

Jacquie perceived that colour prejudicial language flows in the bloodstream of society and in church. She was looking for a space where her experience would be articulated and theologically reflected on, where like-minded people, Black and White, would jointly fight against racism. She was looking for a version of the Benetton Posse in her church. It was a diocesan course, *Seeds of Hope*, that created a space for her. She found what other Black people had said about the course to be true: 'Usually there is a gap between the church and the real world. We cannot discuss our real life in a church context. The *Seeds of Hope* study pack for the first time gave us the opportunity to share our pain about racism in a church context.'[8] After doing *Seeds of Hope* Jacquie was looking for more. The new opportunity came when her vicar, the vicar of All Saints Church, called Jacquie one day to tell her about a 10-week diocesan course in Black and Asian Liberation Theology. It sounded ideal.

'This new course gave me all the nourishment I needed,' Jacquie remembered. 'The words used during the course were soothing. The readings from the Bible and other literature were healing. During the course we as a group felt replenished. This

"Benetton Posse" was a great mix of male and female, Black, White and Asian people. It was extremely good to break down and confirm certain aspects of the Bible such as the myth of Jesus being a White man with blonde hair or how women are second to men.'

She felt proud to be Black, British and a woman, but found English terminology confusing. The English language made her feel that being Black was nothing to be proud of: 'For example, "You are a disgrace to your family, a real black sheep." Or "White Witches are good, pure, kind and will help you, whilst, Black Witches are bad, wicked, evil and ugly too!" It would appear that everything that is black (according to the English Language) is wicked, evil and ugly and anything white is pure, innocent and beautiful.'

During the Black and Asian Liberation Theology course Jacquie and her fellow students found that *The New Oxford Dictionary of English*[9] lists 36 negative uses of the term black: black magic, blackmail, black spot, black sheep are a few. Words pertaining to black or dark are usually deemed as bad and evil. Only in banking terms is it good to be 'in the black'. The meanings given under 'white' are mostly positive.[10] Jacquie began to understand why all her life the usage of the terms black and white have been hurting her so deeply. These terms are used 'to ennoble or condemn, augment or detract, glorify or demean' different groups of people.[11]

Here I give some examples from everyday life. One of my sons is an actor. When he was studying in the Birmingham School of Speech and Drama, one day the students were asked to use the nursery rhyme 'Baa, Baa, black sheep'. They were learning about how the sound of a word relates to the meaning of the word. A student said, 'Doesn't the word black sound evil?' My other son is an artist. He showed me two pots of paints he had just bought. The black container reads, 'black as silent as death' and the white one, 'white pure incarnate'. A Black woman recalled that one day a White clergyman said to her, 'God made Black people to show White people their dark side.'

When you are surrounded by the negative use of the terms black and dark and you yourself are referred to as a black or a dark person, it is a small wonder that many Black people have low self-esteem. Jacquie is proud to be Black, but accessing that pride has not been an easy task. A Black person needs to perform psychological gymnastics to feel proud of their blackness. Most church people are completely unaware that their negative use of the term black continuously undermines the work Black people are doing to feel proud of their colour.

Jacquie's story started with her anger against her friend Trevor when he called her 'nigger'. In Black and Asian theology class Jacquie accessed her pain and then her anger. She knew how her anger on that occasion and many others came from very deep pain. A session on *han* helped her to reflect on her anger. The words of a Korean feminist theologian Chung Hyun Kyung used in the class meant a lot to Jacquie. She quoted them in her story in the belief that many will relate to these words:

> *Han* is a very peculiar feeling. *Han* is the suppressed, amassed and condensed experience of oppression caused by mischief or misfortune so that it forms a kind of lump in ones spirit. This is the typical, prevailing feeling of the Korean people. *Han* is a sense of unresolved resentment against injustice suffered, a sense of helplessness because of the overwhelming odds against us, a feeling of total abandonment (Why hast thou forsaken me?), a feeling of acute pain of sorrow in ones guts and bowels making the whole body writhe and wiggle, and an obstinate urge to take 'revenge' and to right the wrong all these constitute. The feeling of *Han* comes from the sinful interconnections of classism, racism, sexism, colonialism, neo-colonialism and cultural imperialism which Korean people experience everyday.[12]

An experience of oppression creates pain and the pain generates frustration and anger; in short, this is *han*. Jacquie was able to connect her *han* with the *han* of oppressed people all over the world. However, in the Black theology class she was left with not pain and anger, but healing. Jacquie learned the hard way that 'blows are unkind and words can wound too'. In the class she saw that words could also heal and protect. She now thinks it would be more apt to say, 'Words can wound and words can cure.'

Jacquie was healed by seeing that the Bible is not colour prejudiced in the same way as the English language. Black colour hardly ever has any negative significance in the Bible. Darkness is not really a colour term; it is about injustice, suffering, chaos, gloom etc. The First Letter of John 2:9 is an example: 'Whoever says, "I am in the light," while hating a brother or sister, is still in the darkness.' Moreover, darkness is not solely negative, sometimes it is positive in the Bible. According to Exodus 20:21, 1 Kings 8:12, 2 Chronicles 6:1, God dwells in thick darkness. The colour of Satan is not black it is like light or a flash of lightning (Luke 10:18; 2 Cor. 11:14).

When students were asked whether they had ever seen a

picture of Jesus carrying a black lamb, the answer was no. In English 'black sheep' has a negative connotation. This connotation comes from the secular world yet it influences Christian paintings and symbolism. In the Bible a black sheep has no negative symbolism. Genesis 30:32–40 are the only verses in the Bible that talk about the colour of lambs and the colour is black. White sheep or lambs are never mentioned in the Bible. According to Genesis 30 Jacob increased the black and spotted animals particularly lambs and discouraged the growth of the others. This shows that black lambs were considered superior in biblical times.

In Song of Songs 1:5, the woman is black and beautiful. Revelation 6:8 associates not black, but pale green with death: 'I looked and there was a pale green horse! Its rider's name was Death.' Sometimes white has a positive connotation in the Bible, but not always. In the Bible 'as white as snow' is generally negative. In Leviticus 13:3, 4, 10, 13, 16, 17, 19, 20, 21, 24, 25, 26, 38, 39, 42, 43, altogether in 16 verses, and in Exodus 4:6, Numbers 12:10 and 2 Kings 5:27 diseased skin is white and sometimes 'as snow'. White sepulchre and whitewash are negative terms in the Bible. Sometimes European interpreters have read black and white colours into the texts when they are not there. At other times they have given prejudicial meanings to these terms.[13]

After reclaiming relevant biblical verses Jacquie felt better equipped to resist the colour prejudice that is perpetuated through the English language. She said: 'Sometimes, in the past, I let myself feel slightly inferior and consciously excluded myself from the rest of the congregation. I slipped in and out of the door, retaining my silence. But now at my church there is a growing number of Black people, which I am happy about. I am overcoming my shell-like attitude by making myself talk and smile. I say what I believe and it's all right if no one agrees. I pray without ceasing. Sometimes we share a joke or two and I soon lighten up.'

In February 2004, after finishing her course, Jacquie wanted to share some insights from Black and Asian Theology at an 'All-Age Worship Service' in All Saints Church. Jacquie led the service together with the vicar and his wife. Jacquie's own words picture that service: 'It was so exciting to talk about something I feel so passionate about. Sharing the information with the rest of the congregation was awesome. There were nods and smiles from some, concentration on faces from others. We incorporated clips from *Star Trek*; talked about Black historical figures, light and darkness in the Bible and lots more. At the end of the service some members of the congregation said they had been enlightened by the information. Some said that they hadn't been aware of how some everyday English terms can be so offensive.'

Racism is perpetuated in churches not because church people are racist, but because they are unaware. Unconsciously people perpetuate racism. When people go through awareness-building exercises scales fall from their eyes and they begin to see. Seeing is a first step towards changing. Jacquie was able to make people in the congregation see a little of her experience and some White people that day were able to stand a little in Jacquie's shoes. Describing her wonderful experience she wrote, 'I felt a connection that day, greater than before.'

Jacquie concluded her story by saying: 'Jesus understands what it is like to be looked down on and despised; he knows how hurt we are when we are stereotyped in a negative sense. Jesus loves us all equally. The conclusion I have come to is whether you are black, white, pink, yellow (or any shade in between), male, female, adult, child, European, African, Indian – we are loved as an individual. Being one of the "Black Sheep" in the family of God is a privilege indeed; I will do all I can to share the God-given knowledge that has been entrusted to me. My hope is that other members of the flock will follow too.'

11
God's Community of Resistance

The Reality of Crime
What is a crime?
It is a non-conformity to the dominant – be it rules, regulations
  or culture
Does that mean I am committing a crime?
    I'm BLACK
I cannot conform to the dominant facet of this culture,
Is that why you have sentenced me to this life of
    Inequality, of oppression, of drowning, of killing me from
    within
        STOP!
        THINK!
        What is your crime?

Your crime is against me and my brothers,
Your crime is against humanity
    – God's humanity –
What is your sentence?
Re-address yourself, question those crime statistics?
How dare you judge me and impose your justice
How dare you assume the air of self-righteousness?
        STOP!
Are there any statistics for <u>YOUR</u> crime? No
I bet there isn't, my inquiries do not show so who is to know.
    Yes!
I hurt and I sentence you to a lifetime of getting to know me
To love and to being my brother in Christ,
    ENOUGH OF YOUR RHETORIC, ENOUGH!
The issue here is a partnership, equality

WHAT COULD BE SIMPLER?
The dream is mine, but, it belongs to us all
My faith is in God
The reality is ours through Christ.[1]

Sharon Palmer

In 1963 at a very young age Mr Vanico James came to England with his family from the island of Nevis. His parents and most of the brothers and sisters have now gone back and are doing very well in Nevis. Some of his relations there are teachers, leading lawyers and well-respected people.

There is a popular myth that Britain is swamped by people coming from the Commonwealth. However, Vanico's family provides evidence to support government statistics that there is not only an inflow of people but also a constant outflow. 'The number of people leaving the UK to live elsewhere increased slightly from 359,000 in 2002 to a record 362,000 in 2003. The outflow of New Commonwealth citizens increased over the same period. The Old Commonwealth includes Australia, Canada, New Zealand and South Africa. The New Commonwealth includes all other Commonwealth countries.'[2]

Most of Vanico's family have now left the UK, but Vanico has not. Every two years he visits Nevis and finds it refreshing to see Black role models everywhere. He also notices a Christian spirit in Nevis. Vanico wonders whether one day he will return to Nevis, but at present England is his home and he works in a printing company in Birmingham. At work he has to cope with people's stereotypes. A few years ago when he became a trade union representative Vanico did not expect to find racism even in the Union, but he did. Some people who thought of him as a docile Black man were surprised to see him in this role. Some of the White members of the Union were not very happy about a Black man leading and representing them. There is another union representative who is of double heritage. Like Vanico he is also an Anglican. His passion, seriousness and skill in speech give Vanico courage to use his gifts more boldly.

The term 'double heritage' mentioned above needs clarification. A person whose parents are from two different cultures is often called a mixed-race person and sometimes, worse still, a half-caste. These need to be replaced by other terms such as double or dual heritage or multiple heritage. The term mixed-race perpetuates the myth that there are many races.

> Race, as is now widely acknowledged, is a social and political construct, not a biological and genetic fact. It cannot be used scientifically to account for the wide range of differences among peoples. There is more genetic variation within any one so-called race than there is between 'races'. In reality the

human species shares a common gene pool, and a particular genetic combination is to be found in any large population.[3]

Science today has proved what the Bible had always affirmed, that there is one race, the human race. All people are created in God's image and they come from the same root, in biblical language Adam and Eve. Now it is wrong, misleading and even dangerous to talk about mixed race.

The term 'half-caste' is even more offensive than 'mixed race'. Here it is worth quoting a Methodist Minister, Inderjit Bhogal of Kenyan-Indian origin, whose wife is White British. Soon after commencing her first school, their daughter Anjuli came from school one day and said, 'Someone called me a half-caste today.' Inderjit said to her: 'You are not a half child. You are fully human, a whole person ... In your case, because your mum and dad come from two different colours and cultures, you are a doubly blessed child and you carry within you a double heritage. So you are a richer child. Don't let any one give you the idea that you are half this or half that. If they do, tell them you have a double heritage.' Some time after this, one day Inderjit heard Anjuli, who was with a group of friends, correcting one saying, 'No not half-caste, double heritage'. Suddenly all her friends – one with Welsh mother and English father, another with Anglican mother and Roman Catholic father – began to claim that they were double heritage. Inderjit observed, 'A negative concept had been turned into something positive to take pride in.'[4]

A person of multiple identities should be encouraged to take pride in all aspects of their heritage. Christians need to reinforce that self-pride. Such people are then more likely to become an in-spiration to others, as the trade union representative was to Vanico. After speaking about the Union, Vanico spoke about his experience of the church.

Vanico has not always been an Anglican. Originally he was from the Church of the First Born. Now he is a regular member of the Church of England, but from time to time he attends Free Black Churches both in Nevis and here. He is delighted to notice some positive changes taking place in these churches. There used to be strict dress codes for attending church, but now things are much more relaxed. He also notices that many leaders in Free Churches offer voluntary service to the church. This means that often these leaders are highly qualified and have professional secular jobs and their horizon is broad. In their professional capacities they become politically aware of the world issues, particularly Black issues. These social issues they connect with their faith. Since they are conscious of the need for Black awareness movements, during their teaching and preaching they emphasise Black people's honourable past and their biblical heritage. These teachings are empowering for Black people. Vanico realises why the younger generation feels more attracted to these Free Churches than to the established historical churches. Robert Beckford also observes: 'The worshipping tradition ensures that the Black Church is one of the only safe spaces where Black identities are celebrated and perpetuated. For many, the Church is a place of affirmation and empowerment.'[5]

In 1989 Vanico joined an Anglican church. When he started going to this church he heard about its recent history. At one point the congregation had dwindled and the church was about to close. The vicar went to visit the local area inhabited by mostly Black people. He told them in community gatherings that the church was there for them. These people came in and rescued the church.

When Black people started worshipping in the church they were amazed to see specially reserved pews which the rich had at one time bought or rented. Long after that practice ended, still those pews were seen as reserved for certain people, and if any Black person sat there they were moved to the back pews. In Vanico's church some Black churchwardens began to question this custom and removed the old nameplates from the pews, thus making all the pews accessible to all people.

During the interview Vanico gave me a bit of historical information about reserved pews that I did not have before. One issue that played a big part behind the origin of the Free Methodist Church

> was the widespread practice of renting and selling church pews, thus relegating the poor to benches in the back of the sanctuary. 'Free' Methodists called for free seats for all and emphasized tithes and offerings to support the church's ministries ... In 1860, in western New York and Illinois, the Free Methodist Church came into being.'[6]

I am not aware of such organised movements in the Anglican Church. Showing favouritism to the rich is a direct contradiction to some biblical passages, yet it has been an integral part of life and worship in the Church of England. Two years ago in a Network Event I led a discussion on the following verses:

My brothers and sisters, do you with your acts of favouritism really believe in our glorious Lord Jesus Christ? For if a person with gold rings and in fine clothes comes into your assembly, and if a poor person in dirty clothes also comes in, and if you take notice of the one wearing the fine clothes and say, 'Have a seat here, please,' while to the one who is poor you say, 'Stand there,' or, 'Sit at my feet,' have you not made distinctions among yourselves, and become judges with evil thoughts? Listen, my beloved brothers and sisters. Has not God chosen the poor in the world to be rich in faith and to be heirs of the kingdom that he has promised to those who love him? But you have dishonoured the poor. Is it not the rich who oppress you? Is it not they who drag you into court? Is it not they who blaspheme the excellent name that was invoked over you? … But if you show partiality, you commit sin and are convicted by the law as transgressors. (James 2:1–9)

Discussing the Letter of James, a Latin American biblical scholar, Elsa Tamez, writes: 'I know of churches where the letter is skipped over in the liturgies because there are many rich members in the congregation, and it is very uncomfortable to speak against them when they are sitting in the front seats.'[7] At the Network Event I asked people whether they had ever heard these verses read out in their church. The unanimous answer was 'no'. During the lunch at that event a Black member showed me the pews that used to be reserved for the rich and told me, 'See why the verses from St James are skipped over.'

At Vanico's church, although some Black churchwardens took down the nameplates from reserved pews, a residue of this reserved pews mindset remains among some White church members. Very recently a White member asked somebody to move from a pew claiming that it was her place. This incident was discussed in the PCC (Parochial Church Council) meeting and steps were taken to stop such things. The Letter of James can help Anglican churches to examine whether they have established a tradition of favouritism to the upper class in the very heart of the worship.

Vanico's church is now a predominantly Black church; however, a few White people who have moved outside the parish still return to worship there. Sometimes Vanico realises how different a White person's vantage point is from a Black person's and how people's distinct perspectives influence their understanding of faith. He gave examples of some church-related activities where

Black people's thinking seemed to clash with some White people's concepts.

After watching on the media the sufferings of some people in South Africa, Black people in the congregation proposed fasting and all-night prayer in their church. They also intended that after the prayer money would be collected to give to South Africa. Some White people felt very unhappy about it. They said that they would pray, but not give money. Church money was for their church and not for South Africa. Moreover, who knows whether the South Africans would not use their money to kill White people? Eventually Black people won the debate and money was sent to South Africa.

Vanico is a member of a Justice and Peace Committee. A White person came to speak about asylum-seekers and told people how the wealth and economic power of Britain today is directly connected with the past and present exploitation of the poor countries. Although it came from a fellow White person it was still very difficult for some White people to hear it. They were unable to see the part the West had played and is playing in creating today's world poverty and large-scale migration of the poor. Christians who should be ahead of others in challenging what is wrong usually fall behind. But western sociology, literature, history and anthropology do engage with the issues connected with racism.[8] Peter Fryer looks at some historical documents regarding Britain's part in the slave trade and quotes the merchant Joshua Gee who wrote in 1729:

> The supplying our Plantations with Negroes is of that extraordinary Advantage to us ... Plantations ... are the great Cause of the Increase of the Riches of the Kingdom ... All this great Increase of our Treasure proceeds chiefly from the Labour of Negroes in the Plantations.[9]

Fryer continues:

> Funds accumulated from the triangular trade helped to finance James Watt's steam engine, the south Wales iron and coal industries, the south Yorkshire iron industry, the north Wales slate industry, the Liverpool and Manchester Railway, and the Great Western Railway. Rising British capitalism had a magic money machine, an endless chain with three links: sugar cultivation; manufacturing industry; and the slave trade.[10]

In short, colonialism and the slave trade contributed towards the wealth, the economic and political power that Britain enjoys today.

The speaker at the Justice and Peace meeting was reminding people that most of the British population are still reaping the fruits of Britain's past imperialism and therefore have an obligation towards the poor who seek asylum. Vanico was shocked to see a White social worker who works with the homeless disputing what the speaker had said. Instead of expressing empathy the social worker was talking about bogus asylum-seekers and how detrimental it was for Britain to welcome these people. James Cone writes:

> There are Whites who say that they do not owe Blacks anything because they did not enslave anybody, did not segregate or lynch anybody, and are not White supremacists ... At an individual level, there is some common sense truth about that observation. But if you benefit from the past and present injustices committed against Blacks, you are partly and indirectly accountable ... as a member of the institutions that perpetuate racism. We cannot just embrace what is good ... and ignore the bad. We must accept the responsibility to do everything we can to correct ... past and present wrongs.[11]

Vanico had immediate empathy with the asylum-seekers and realised that as a Black person he has a particular perspective on issues in British society, different from that of many White people.

Vanico is a Lay Reader. He feels restricted by the set readings to preach on. It is difficult for him to relate these biblical passages with the current issues that he feels passionate about. However, sometimes he is able to make connections with contemporary concerns and preach on the sufferings of Black people in the area. Talking about such things makes Vanico passionate and he expresses his emotion in his preaching. After one such passionate outburst a White man might say to him things such as: 'White preachers do not do these things, do they? We are Anglicans here.' Displaying passion and emotion come naturally to Vanico, a Black man. A White man who is culturally conditioned to keep 'a stiff upper lip' presumes that all Anglicans should behave in the same way and puts pressure on Vanico to conform.

Vanico notices how some White people have two standards, one for the White and one for the Black people. White people who support western governments when they go to war still advise Black people to turn the other cheek and be non-violent in the face of oppression. These people do not have an answer to Vanico's question, 'Why didn't Jesus turn his other cheek when he was struck?' (see John 18:21–23). In the UK and beyond, Black people are frequently asked by White people to turn the other cheek. James Cone states: 'We have had too much of white love, the love that tells blacks to turn the other cheek and go the second mile.'[12] Vanico knows that the verses about turning the other cheek and going the second mile in Matthew 5:38–41 and Luke 6:29 have been misused by Christians to keep oppressed people docile.

Walter Wink challenges the traditional interpretation and argues that these passages have

> become the basis for systematic training in cowardice, as Christians are taught to acquiesce to evil. Cowardice is scarcely a term one associates with Jesus. Either he failed to make himself clear, or we have misunderstood him. There is plenty of cause to believe the latter.

Wink then raises many pertinent questions. In Jesus' culture the right hand was usually used for slapping and a right-handed slap could not strike the right cheek of anybody. So why did Jesus advise the person struck on the right cheek to turn the other cheek? When a person was sued and their outer garment demanded in payment, why did Jesus ask the person to give the undergarment as well? The Roman soldiers could impose only limited forced labour, one mile, on the Jews. Why did Jesus tell them to go the second mile? Wink concludes that Jesus taught people to resist evil in many different ways with their soul power. (It is not possible to include the full discussion here, but the interested reader might like to look at Wink's interpretation of these passages.[13]) Vanico objects to glib and unthinking use of Jesus' teaching to 'turn the other cheek' and 'go the second mile'.

During the study of *Seeds of Hope* again Vanico noticed White people's double standard when they advised Black people to forget the past and put the memory of oppression behind them. Yet every 11th of November the same people have Remembrance Day with all its grandeur to remember their own sufferings. It is actually futile to tell Black people to forget past oppression, for example the history of slavery. It is psychologically impossible for them. Stanley Cohen argues that oppressed people 'may have phases of forgetting or denial, but most of them, most of the time … are quite unable to shut out their memories'. Cohen goes on to say: 'Slow cultural forgetting works best when powerful forces have an interest in keeping people quiet.' When White people ask Black people to forget their past, it becomes obvious that they are the powerful and they have a vested interest in silencing Black people. Moreover, repressing the past is psychologically as well as politically dangerous for human groups. 'This is what Archbishop Tutu means about the past coming back to haunt you.'[14]

The Bible does not ask oppressed people to forget their past. At the celebration of the Passover meal, Hebrew people were – and the Jews of today are – asked to remember that they were slaves in Egypt. In the context of the Passover Jesus established the Eucharist and asked his followers to eat the bread and drink the wine in remembrance of his death on the cross. Instead of teaching us to forget, the Bible urges us to remember. Moreover, the crucial point of the biblical concept of remembrance lies in its 'why' and 'how'. There are many verses in the Bible such as the following: 'You shall not wrong or oppress a resident alien, for you were aliens in the land of Egypt' (Exod. 22:21). If groups remember their past oppression rightly, they treat the present oppressed groups justly. Vanico is close to the biblical teachings when he remembers the past sufferings of Black people and has empathy for the asylum-seekers of today.

Although Vanico observes that generally White people have a vantage point which is different from his own, he knows that all White people are not the same. There are a few who are aware of Black people's sufferings and they articulate things eloquently and passionately. For example, there is a woman in his church who in her secular professional career has been well versed in racism awareness issues. When somebody in church talks about 'coloured people', she is the first one to object. (The term 'coloured' lost favour among Black people during the 1960s Black Power Movement and was superseded by 'Black'. It is now regarded as offensive.[15]) Instead of listening, some White people argue with her and give the impression that a White person must not side with Black people.

Vanico has been to many Black people's gatherings and listened to speeches given by Black scholars, such as the Old Testament Professor Randall Bailey. He has also studied a Black Theology course in the diocese. He said, 'Previously in some Free Churches I was given crumbs and felt proud to be Black but when I listened to Professor Bailey or did the Black Theology course I knew that I was fed real food. These helped me to stand tall.' These theological experiences made Vanico realise that although the teachings in Free Black Churches affirmed his identity, he needed a kind of Black theological grounding that was still lacking there. He compared the affirmation of his Black identity with crumbs and Black theological grounding with real food.

Vanico believes that most churches are still not doing enough for Black young people who are building their self-esteem on the basis of Black music such as rap and hip-hop. He recognises that much in Black music is wholesome, spiritual and theological. These cultural expressions build Black young people up. Yet more is needed. According to Vanico, Black music is good, but it is like beefburgers. Established churches are denying young people the steak they need for their identity, spirituality and theology. So they are living on beefburgers. Vanico has studied Black Theology and he knows how that has nourished him. White led churches often deny Black people this nourishment. The church leaders who do not know anything about Black Theology are the first ones to give a verdict on this theology. They discourage their members, saying that Black Theology is divisive and creates unnecessary problems. Paul Grant observed some White people's arrogance: 'I saw plainly the appalling arrogance of those who believe that their "understanding" allows them the right to define exactly what is right and wrong for people they don't know in situations of which they have no experience.'[16] Vanico knows that church leaders' stereotypical ideas about Black Theology do not match the reality.

He states that because of the lack of steak, Black young people leave the established churches. By steak he means a kind of spirituality that resists and counters oppression. This concept of spirituality is found in the words of Robert Beckford:

> Spirituality here is understood as the way in which God goes about the process of holistic liberation in this world. Liberation is also God's redemptive work, concerned with every aspect of human existence. The Church must therefore be a place whose very spirituality ensures that it is God's community of resistance.[17]

12
Watching You

Veneration of the Cross
I cannot venerate the glorification of unnecessary suffering,
but I can venerate all those who work to alleviate suffering
and bring its causes to judgement.

I cannot venerate violence and victimization,
but I can venerate the forces of life
that resist the forces of death and destruction.

I cannot venerate the cross as somehow uniquely sacred,
but I can venerate all who die with dignity, courage and trust
and name them each as holy, God-bearing, grace-filled persons.

As I take the cross in my hands and kiss it,
I am committing myself,
not to sacrificial suffering, but to the struggle for life
which nevertheless has to wrestle
with the forces of death and destruction and hostility.
I am saying I am willing to be engaged in that struggle and to pay
    its cost.

I am choosing life with open eyes,
I am cognisant of the cost such a choice may demand.
I am aligning myself with all who work for justice, peace and
    liberation.
I am placing myself on the side of life.

Christ whose cross has been used and abused
to justify slavery, the abuse of women, the misery of the poor:
Make us strong to resist every exploitation of another
and ready to pay the cost of the struggle for life.[1]

Nicola Slee

The previous chapters are stories of people whose home is Britain. In this chapter the storytellers are short-term residents. They are in an advantageous position, because they can look at both British society and their own at the same time.

The Revd Beatrice Gill from Belize in Central America spent a year from 2003 to 2004 in an Anglican church in Birmingham. When she heard about this book she let me have some of the sermons that she had preached in that church and allowed me to use extracts from them.

'Who controls the past controls the future: who controls the present controls the past.'[2] This means that those who dominate our world at present are in a position to write our histories; and as long as they write our histories they control our futures. Beatrice dreams of a future different from the one set in motion by Christopher Columbus. The European-American historians usually glorify Columbus. They write this history with a dominant hand to control the future of the oppressed. Beatrice desires a future for the power-less uncontrolled by the powerful. In order to unleash this future, in her sermon she put forward a version of history from the perspective of the oppressed.

'I invite you', she said, 'to take a look at the past activities in this area where I come from. My country is now poor. How did it become poor? When Columbus sailed across the Atlantic to discover the new world he found a people with a history of achievements, with a kingdom of Mayas, Aztecs, Incas, Arawaks and Carib Indians. It is estimated that the population in Central America and the Caribbean at the time was around 70 to 90 million people. That indigenous population today is reduced to just over 3.5 million people. Columbus saw religious monuments, which, it is said, were built more skilfully than the pyramids of Egypt. He saw various inventions to assist the people in their struggle against nature. There were various works of art. He met astronomers and was introduced to a number system which included the concept of zero. He saw developed systems of irrigation and agriculture. This great civilization was unknown to the newcomers.

'The coming of Columbus in the wake of the Capitalist mercantile exploitations was an event that was to destroy this region and reduce it to poverty. I would like to draw your attention to the terrible genocide which occurred in Jamaica. In 1494 Columbus discovered the island of Jamaica and the people who lived there – the Arawak Indians. The estimated population was 60,000. The British captured Jamaica from Spain in 1655 and at that time the population of the Arawak Indians was zero.'

Beatrice is not alone in understanding the curse brought by Columbus to the whole region of Central America, the Caribbean and beyond. In 2002 I visited the Dominican Republic. A guide book affirmed what I found there: 'In the modern-day Dominican Republic, superstitious souls prefer not to mention the name of Columbus, for it is widely reputed to carry a *fuku* – a curse.'[3] However, Black scholars know that the curse is not in the mentioning but in the glorifying of the name. They tell the truth without fear, knowing only the truth will liberate people. Hilary Beckles writes:

> It was accepted by colonial whites that the march towards economic development required the systematic enslavement of human beings. There was a clearly formulated view that it was necessary, morally legitimate, not only to enslave persons, but also to exterminate people in an attempt to confiscate lands.[4]

The policies of colonisation, enslavement and extermination of non-White people, which were inaugurated by Columbus, went on for at least four hundred years in different parts of the world.

There is enough evidence to prove that, starting from Columbus, the European colonisers adopted the policy of extermination of people whom they considered inferior beings. I give a few examples from British records. As late as 1851 Herbert Spencer, a philosopher, pointed out 'that the "purifying process" by which animals killed off the sick, deformed, and old was at work in human society too, thanks to the "decrees of a large, far-reaching benevolence".' In 1862 John Arthur Roebuck, MP for Sheffield, told the House of Commons that in New Zealand 'the Englishmen would destroy the Maori, and the sooner the Maori are destroyed the better'. '*Social Evolution* (1894) by Benjamin Kidd, a minor civil servant, made its author famous and sold 250,000 copies. It caught the popular imagination with its praise of the "vigorous and virile" Anglo-Saxon race, in mere contrast with whom the weaker, "inferior" races tended to die off.'[5] Peter Fryer reminds us:

> It should be borne in mind that racial extinction was not just a matter of theory. The black people of Tasmania did not long survive the invasion of their island by the dominant race. They were hunted down without mercy. The last of them died in 1869. And racist ideology justified genocide. Social Darwinism

taught white people that the Tasmanians were their brothers and sisters. It also taught them that the extermination of their brothers and sisters was an inevitable part of the struggle for existence, in which their own 'superior' race alone was destined to survive.[6]

Although the European colonisers claimed that they were killing off the inferior 'races', Beatrice asserted that the colonised people were highly civilised. A Dominican priest, Bartolome de las Casas, kept a journal of the devastation caused by the invasion of Columbus. After a few years of the arrival of Columbus, de las Casas came to the devastated region and wrote of the Arawaks:

> of all the infinite universe of humanity, these people are the most guileless, the most devoid of wickedness and duplicity ... yet into this sheepfold ... there came some Spaniards who immediately behaved like ravening beasts ... Their reason for killing and destroying ... is that Christians have an ultimate aim which is to acquire gold.[7]

A historian Howard Zinn laments:

> Yes, all over the islands of Hispaniola, where he [Columbus], his brothers, his men, spent most of their time, he erected crosses. But also, all over the island, they built gallows – 340 of them by the year 1500. Crosses and gallows – that deadly historic juxtaposition.[8]

Since Columbus himself, the Dominican priest Bartolome de las Casas and many others kept their diaries, the unpalatable history of European expansion is not lost. But this history has been covered up so that the Europeans and the North Americans can profit from past wrongs without being challenged. The past is directly connected with the present.

> Without the colonial Caribbean's role within the North Atlantic system there would have been no eighteenth century Industrial Revolutions; without the colonial Caribbean there would have been no European commercial ascendancy in the nineteenth century; without the colonial Caribbean there would have been no early twentieth century global financial order; it was the foundation upon which the present dispensation was built.[9]

Like Beatrice, many of the oppressed of the world have now woken up to see how the past is controlling the present. They demand that the West stops reaping the harvest of the past wrongs, so that the people of colour, the poor of the world, can simply live once more. Beatrice tried to share her pain with her Christian brothers and sisters in Birmingham, hoping that they would begin to see the world not only from the viewpoint of the powerful, but from that of the powerless. At this point in history we Black people are not expecting an overnight reversal of the world order; all we hope is that White Christians would try to see how we understand the world. That seeing itself is a turning point, which we are eagerly awaiting. Beatrice saw very little signs of this turning point. Mostly she received only arguments from White people who said that they were not responsible for what their ancestors did. Either silence or arguments are the automated reactions we Black people regularly receive from our White brothers and sisters. Automated in the sense that we can always predict the responses. James Baldwin tries to see what might be going on in the minds of White people:

> Most people are not naturally reflective any more than they are naturally malicious, and the white man prefers to keep the black man at a certain human remove because it is easier for him thus to preserve his simplicity and avoid being called to account for crimes committed by his forefathers, or his neighbors. He is inescapably aware, nevertheless, that he is in a better position in the world than the black men are ... People who shut their eyes to reality simply invite their own destruction, and anyone who insists on remaining in a state of innocence long after that innocence is dead turns himself into a monster.[10]

Some White people desperately try to silence this painful history and they believe that they can achieve this by keeping Black people 'at a certain human remove'. Beatrice noticed that even after she had been with the congregation for eight months, many still kept her at a distance. During her sermon she told the congregation, 'Some people I meet in the shops and I get excited, I see a face I recognise from church and I look over to smile and share a greeting. But the person looks away and I pass by with words unspoken.'

Europeans often pretend that if they close their eyes to Black people and their pain, they can continue to enjoy all the privileges that have been bestowed on them by their past unpleasant history. Franz Fanon addresses the European world:

> The Third World does not mean to organize a great crusade of

hunger against the whole of Europe. What it expects from those who for centuries have kept it in slavery is that they will help it to rehabilitate mankind [*sic*], and make man [*sic*] victorious everywhere, once and for all. But it is clear that we are not so naive as to think that this will come about with the cooperation and the goodwill of the European governments. This huge task which consists of reintroducing mankind into the world, the whole of mankind, will be carried out with the indispensable help of the European peoples, who themselves must realize that in the past they have often joined the ranks of our common masters where colonial questions were concerned. To achieve this the European peoples must first decide to wake up and shake themselves, use their brains, and stop playing the stupid game of the Sleeping Beauty.[11]

Beatrice based her sermon on Jesus' commandment in John 13:34–35. As Judas went out to betray Jesus, Jesus said: 'I give you a new commandment, that you love one another. Just as I have loved you, you also should love one another. By this everyone will know that you are my disciples, if you have love for one another.' The betrayed people of the Two-Thirds World are asking the European-American Christian world to show once more the power of love instead of the love of power. It is very encouraging to see that, together with the world's poor, European-American Christians are playing a big role in the Jubilee 2000 debt cancellation and Make Poverty History movements (2005). This proves that they are the disciples of Jesus Christ. However, the colour of world poverty is black. The countries with Black people are the poorest. If the connections between economic and race issues are not spelt out courageously, these movements will lose something of the power that can change the oppressive world order.

Beatrice spoke about economic injustice. Besides her, two other short-term residents spoke about various things they have observed in Birmingham. Dorn Henry, a woman in her twenties from St Kitts, is doing an MA in Applied Community Studies. The Revd Isaiah Phillip, also from St Kitts, is a PhD student in Birmingham. One common theme in their comments on life in Britain was the sense of being mistrusted. Both of them observed that in general White people, whether Christian or not, presume that Black people are trying to cheat. Coming from abroad they notice it more, because in their home country they had never faced such a lack of trust. Black people cheat no more than White people. If there is a general presumption that Black people are cheats, that presumption comes from an oppressor group mentality. This is what oppressor groups generally do: they project wrong onto the oppressed group. Franz Fanon wonders why 'Sin is Negro as virtue is white. All those white men in a group, guns in their hands, cannot be wrong. I am guilty.'[12] Maybe this projection comes from an unconscious guilt feeling. Mary Keller, a White scholar, argues that 'Whiteness has a vested interest in maintaining its self-perception as innocent.'[13]

Dorn, an overseas student, pays much higher fees than home students, yet she receives no student loan. She had to bring enough money to survive before she could get part-time work in the UK. She brought a bank draft from St Kitts to manage for the first few months. In desperate need of cash, she had no access to her own money, because the banks would not open an account for her. They gave the impression that a Black woman could not have so much money unless it was ill-gotten money. One bank refused her and another bank took three months to open an account for her. These harassments taught Dorn that she was now living in a White country and her skin colour made her a suspect.

Soon after that experience she was with a whole group of students getting on a bus. The White driver accused her of not having the right bus pass and was refusing to let her on. That was embarrassing; all eyes were on her. The driver was affirming the stereotypes in people's minds: a Black woman trying to cheat! Luckily her Greek student friend intervened. She said to the driver, 'I have the same kind of bus pass and so do all the students who got on the bus. What makes you stop her?' When challenged, the driver let Dorn get on the bus.

Isaiah believed that because of his skin colour he too was regarded with suspicion. After being in a college for a while Isaiah wanted to bring his family and move to a multicultural area with them. He went to an Anglican church school to book a place for his daughter who was to come in August. The White head teacher said, 'Wait until the daughter comes.' Isaiah said, 'But that would be too late, this is why I need to book a place now.' Although Isaiah had his clerical collar on, the head teacher refused to believe him. She was unfriendly. When Isaiah wanted to look around the school no staff accompanied him. A child showed him around. After receiving this cold reception Isaiah went to look at another Anglican church school nearby. The Black head teacher there behaved completely differently. She was very welcoming and promised a place for his daughter. A member of the staff showed him around. Now the daughter is attending this school.

The irony is Isaiah is now a parish priest and the school that did not welcome his daughter is his parish school. When he started his regular duties as a priest in the school, the head teacher left. Isaiah wonders whether it was too embarrassing for her to stay on there. Isaiah understands that the White head teacher did not want to believe him simply because he is Black.

Beatrice, Dorn and Isaiah all remarked that church life in their home countries is not separated from everyday life. It was therefore nothing out of the ordinary for Beatrice to bring justice issues into her sermons in Birmingham, but that shocked some people in the congregation. Reflecting on their experience in the UK both Dorn and Isaiah became more deeply aware that in their home country church leaders are organic leaders, part of the community. Church people are socially, culturally and politically involved. The church challenges society and society challenges the church.

Isaiah said: 'Here the congregation is small. There is not much connection with the community. I feel shut in the church and realise how I had taken things for granted in St Kitts. Now I appreciate it much more.' In order to connect his community with the church, Isaiah has started to be involved in the Youth Offending Service. He is a member of a Community Panel dealing with first-time offenders. The panel meets them regularly to work things out with them so that they would not offend again. These young people really appreciate that a priest is involved in the panel and they take care not to offend again. The vicars in this multicultural area are delighted to have a Black priest among them. Isaiah builds informal networks in the community and reaches out to people. He is involved in intentional visiting with the aim of attracting lapsed Christians, for example, ex-prisoners, people with mental illness and divorcees. Such people often fall outside a vicar's visiting circle. The message to the ex-prisoners is, 'We give you another chance, keep out of trouble.' Because of his colour Isaiah has an instant connection with the Black community in the neighbour-hood.

Isaiah said that he is puzzled as to why youth work is so dis-connected from church life. Youth ministry is funded by the church, but youth work has other funding. Both Dorn and Isaiah found the sacred and the secular rigidly separated in British society. The Diocesan Youth Council is asking churches to make sure that young people are represented on Parochial Church Councils. But young people are not in the churches; they are in the youth groups. Not much groundwork is being done to bring Christian young people from these groups to the church. Isaiah believes that somebody needs to connect these young people to their worshipping communities. Unless this work is done it is futile to ask churches to find young people for the Parochial Church Councils. Like Sunday school teachers, voluntary youth ministers need to build up young worshipping communities. Some of this work is being done, but more is needed.

Both Dorn and Isaiah reported that in the Caribbean congregations are large, yet still a newcomer is noticed and warmly welcomed. This way big congregations attract people and grow further. Here congregations are small but no interest is shown to the newcomer. Dorn and Isaiah are not surprised that congregations here remain small. Both of them spoke from their experience. When they tried many different churches in Birmingham they were not noticed. Nobody spoke to them and there was no welcome for the newcomer. Two ministers from Dorn's church came to the Anglican Society on the university campus which Dorn also attended. She expected the ministers to acknowledge her, since they had seen her in church, but there was no recognition.

Another short-term resident in Birmingham, Douglas Machiridza, believes that the clergy sometimes play a big role in making newcomers feel welcome. Douglas, his wife Alice and baby Tawana came to the UK in 2002 from Zimbabwe. Douglas is here on a five-year permit as a social worker. When they started attending an Anglican church, the priest ensured that they felt at home and got involved in the activities of the church. Douglas said, 'He sort of knew that if we did not engage in the church activities we would be isolated. I am happy to report that I read in church, my wife helps and I am on the Parish Council. My family and I feel very much at home now in the church.'

Dorn expected such a welcome and was disappointed. In September 2001 she was introduced to a church. There were quite a lot of Black people in that church, yet for the most part White people did everything. A few Black people had roles such as helping with the chalice, but no young people were involved. In the Caribbean Dorn was a parish youth co-ordinators' leader. Herself a young person with all the experience of youth work, Dorn sat in the congregation for ten months. Nobody ever asked her to do a reading or anything. After ten months she was about to leave, when she was asked to help out in Sunday school and do the readings in church. That was too late for her: she was leaving. Some White vicars, instead of being pleased about the presence of Black young people in church, say they do not know what to do with them. Dorn tried another church which was evangelical and child-focused. She said, 'If you were children or the parents of children, the service suited you. But it suited nobody else.'

Back at home her church is charismatic and youth-friendly. A child from five years of age is asked to do things in the church. Everybody is invited to participate. Here in the UK the age barrier is noticeable. Churches in the Caribbean are connected with the larger community; they are also ecumenical. Denominations are not so rigidly separated from each other as they are here. People mix and mingle and learn from each other.

Dorn said quite a bit about how it is to be a Black young person in the Caribbean and how it must be for Black young people here. She is very aware of gender and colour issues. She explained how that awareness grew. When she was much younger she noticed gender inequality at home. Girls did much more work in the house than the boys. Dorn had important school examinations and could not tolerate this discrimination. She gave an ultimatum: 'If you want me to be successful at school, change this way of running home or I leave.' Things changed. The experience of oppression taught Dorn that there were inequalities in society, and made her aware that challenging is a good thing. Discriminatory practices do not change unless challenged.

She also became politically aware of colour issues at a very young age. When she was 12 years old she already knew about Malcolm X and Martin Luther King. Bob Marley's music was a liberating force for her. Cable television films exposed the wrongs of apartheid in South Africa. Movies made by Africans and African-Americans opened her eyes. She watched *Roots* and became radicalised. Cable television gave her a global perspective. She experienced Christianity as a liberating as well as a consoling power. When things do not change immediately, she is aware that Jesus is consoling her.

The Anglican church in her home country took care of her whole being. She was able to know what is right and what is wrong. For example she was brought up to know not to swear. Boundaries were set when she was very young and that later on gave her greater freedom. Now she does not have to waste her energy by being constantly anxious about what is right or wrong. She has more time and energy left to get on with life and achieve positive things. She appreciates the balance between conformity and independence that the Anglican church back at home taught her. She said: 'You are brought up to be a part of your community and church. When you are older you reap the benefit of conforming at a young age. But you are allowed to have a free mind to think for yourself.'

She continued: 'Here in the UK there are no boundaries for young people. People constantly call good bad and bad good. Here my advice to British people is, "Listen to what the media don't tell you." The British know more about what it is to be a secular person, but not what it is to be a Christian. Britain was very good at spreading Christianity but it did not keep much of Christianity for itself. The British took our material possessions but gave away the most prized possession, Christianity.'

Dorn also reflected on how difficult it must be for Black young people in the Church of England to affirm their Black identity. She wondered where the space could be found for Black Anglican youth to become aware of their identity. Pete Ward asserts: 'For young people passing through adolescence means that they are in one way or another marginalized. The establishment of a sense of who they are in relation to others is a matter of survival and therefore necessary.'[14] Dorn believes that it is the Church's duty to ensure that Black young people survive well in this White environment by establishing a sense of who they are.

Some Black young people in the UK find their role models only in music and sports. That is not adequate. They need role models in other spheres of life. Dorn was surprised that during Black History month prime time television did not show anything of Black history. Black History month in October was so hidden compared to the Remembrance Day when everybody was wearing poppies. Dorn said that the whole society in the UK is so oppressive that she could not live here very long. Her final comment was, 'Thank God that I was not born in the UK but in the Caribbean. I am going back home to my paradise.'

All the storytellers in this chapter recently crossed geographical and cultural boundaries to come to Britain. This crossing of boundaries deepened their awareness of how some White people perceive themselves and Black people. The storytellers here have offered an outsider's view which might help the insiders to see themselves in a new light. Often certain aspects of truth are exposed at the juncture where outsiders and insiders meet.

Conclusion

A Healing Touch
Who touched me? Somebody touched me
With the needs, the dreams and the hopes of the world
Who touched me? Somebody touched me
And I turned and saw the people
And I turned and listened to their story
Who touched me? Somebody touched me
And I turned and saw two worlds where God created one
And the gates of the rich were closed

And I dreamed of the world you created
A garden with plenty for everyone
With a stream of clean flowing water
For all to drink

And I believe in life
I believe in hope
I believe in a future
Where there is one world
Which we build together.
Who touched me? Somebody touched me
And I pray
Stay with us, Lord, as we work for a better world.
Amen.[1]

Linda Jones

In *Jesus is Dread* Robert Beckford has a very interesting discussion on the role of Black Anglicans in working against racism. Beckford takes account of Malcolm X's views about the 'house Negroes' and the 'field Negroes'. During slavery, a slave working in the field was in a worse condition than the one who worked in the master's house. Malcolm believed that the 'field Negroes' really hated their masters and were involved in a resistance movement against slavery, whereas the 'house Negroes' acquiesced.

In Chapter 5 the Revd Canon Eve Pitts has made use of

Malcolm X's term 'house nigger' to refer to some of her own people who betrayed her. Beckford believes that Malcolm's portrayal of 'house Negroes' was only partially true, because there was another side to their lives. They did not all acquiesce or betray fellow slaves. Like the 'field Negroes' they also resisted slavery, but since they were inside the slave master's house and therefore often in a better position to resist, their strategy was different. Beckford compares Black Anglicans with the 'house Negroes', because they worship 'in the former slave master's Church'. He then shows that Black Anglicans have a viable strategy and in recent years have been very vocal in the struggle against racism. I go along with some of Beckford's arguments and then take the discussion further.[2] I will come back to it a little later.

Remaining very close to the Bible and other historical documents, some theologians of liberation unashamedly declare that the biblical God is God of the oppressed. In choosing the Hebrews, God did not favour an ethnic, but a marginalised group. The term *habiru* is often equated with the word 'Hebrew' and is also spelled *apiru*.

> Egyptian documents of the Empire period (fifteenth to twelfth century) refer to them, both as foes and rebels in Asia and as bondsmen in Egypt ... The term 'Apiru/Hapiru' ... seems to have referred originally not to an ethnic unit but to a stratum in society. This may be argued not only from their wide geographical distribution, but also from the fact that their names, where these are known, do not belong to any one linguistic unit and vary in this regard from region to region. Men of various races and languages might be Apiru. The term apparently denoted a class of people without citizenship, who lived on the fringes of the existing social structure, without roots or fixed place in it.[3]

When the Bible says 'God of the Hebrews', it can equally mean God of the oppressed. The Hebrews were oppressed and marginalised people. They were *anawim*, the poor of Yahweh: 'whether or not they lived in misery, [they] were particularly sensitive to the existence of physical poverty and injustice.'[4] The biblical people were not only an oppressed group of people, they were nomadic people. All Hebrew Jewish people including Jesus would have recited regularly, 'A wandering Aramean was my ancestor; he went down into Egypt and lived there as an alien, few in number, and there he became a great nation, mighty and populous' (Deut. 26:5). The biblical Hebrew people did not build any of the ancient empires; they lived under these empires. During several periods in history they were exiled in foreign lands, thus forming what has become known as the diaspora, Jews living outside Israel. The origin of the term diaspora lies in the Septuagint (Deut. 28:25) in the phrase, 'thou shalt be a dispersion (diaspora) in all the kingdoms of the earth.'[5] God chose these dispersed people.

Jesus Christ, God incarnate, showed us the nature of the divine by choosing the foolish things in the world. He flouted the patriarchal standard and was born of a woman alone. Instead of accepting Herod's palace, he favoured the manger for his birth. Jesus identified with the diaspora: the baby Jesus and his parents were asylum-seekers in Egypt. He was a homeless poor man who had table fellowship with the poor, the sinners and the prostitutes. He was not one of the powerful, but was one hunted down by them. He identified with the innocent sufferers of the world and was tortured at the cruel hand of the Roman Empire. He died on the cross as a criminal. St Paul revealed the heart of the Bible in saying:

> God chose what is foolish in the world to shame the wise; God chose what is weak in the world to shame the strong; God chose what is low and despised in the world, things that are not, to reduce to nothing things that are, so that no one might boast in the presence of God. (1 Cor. 1:27–30)

Black and Asian Anglicans in Britain have much in common with the biblical people. They are on the margins of society struggling for justice. They are also the diaspora. Now this term is applied to all people who are dispersed from their original homeland.[6] Jesus identified with such people who were on the edge of society, but he did not remain with one particular group. He constantly moved to the centre of power to challenge the power structure and then back to the margin. He was always travelling between the Galilee of the poor and the Jerusalem of the establishment. In this process Jesus was breaking down the barriers between the powerful and the powerless and bringing about the Kingdom of God. Jesus was a missionary. Mission comes from the Latin term *missio* meaning send. He was always being sent by God from one group to the other. Christians are also missionaries, they can never settle in any comfort zones.

While the Kingdom of God breaks down barriers between different groups of people, the kingdom of the world bestows privilege on certain groups at the expense of the others. The advantaged groups have many temptations to remain in the centre of power. Slavery, colonialism, racism and neocolonialism have established White people in zones of comfort. A White scholar, Peggy McIntosh, realised:

> I had been taught about racism as something that puts others at a disadvantage, but had been taught not to see one of its corollary aspects, white privilege, which puts me at an advantage. I have come to see white privilege as an invisible package of unearned assets that I can count on cashing in each day, but about which I was 'meant' to remain oblivious.[7]

In her article she gives a list of 46 things that a White person can take for granted which a Black person cannot, from being able to worry about racism without being seen as self-interested or self-seeking to being able to buy 'flesh-coloured' elastoplast that more or less matches one's skin colour. This is not an exhaustive list; one can continue to add things to the list from one's own experience. Inclusion of the full list is beyond the scope of this book, but it would open the eyes of interested readers.[8] If Christians settle in positions of privilege and forget their missionary vocation of constant movement, then those unearned privileges become destructive for them.

When privileged groups internalise the notion that they are superior beings they have an attitude which has been named 'internalised dominance'. 'Internalized dominance is the incorporation of the fact of social privilege into the thought patterns, the behaviour patterns, and the expectations of people in the dominant place.'[9] Internalised dominance socially conditions people. People become so programmed that they see and hear not with biological eyes and ears, but through their belief systems: 'seeing they do not perceive, and hearing they do not listen, nor do they understand' (Matt. 13:13). The stories in this book give several examples of White people showing the symptoms of internalised dominance. Black people are not seen; they are not heard when they greet White people. Through false assumptions, misleading stereotypes and negative body language White people express their racism. The most comical examples come from the experience of Asian Christians. Even after some Asians worshipped together with fellow Christians, and even took part in leading the services, they were asked by White people, 'What religion are you?' White people show many symptoms of internalised dominance, yet they are quite unaware of what they are doing. A White person observes: 'The ways in which our behaviour is oppressive is immediately clear to anyone who is in the target place in relation to us. But as non-target people we experience ourselves as being "ordinary", "just who we are".[10]

David Haslam talks about the hallucinations of pleasantness and well-being that many White people suffer.[11] They often seem to be sleepwalking. While it is quite dangerous for people to sleep-walk, it is equally dangerous for others to be with them. Moreover, since this sleepwalk is caused by social conditioning, it is not complete unawareness. Minds are in the 'twilight between knowing and not-knowing'; 'we seem to have access to reality, but choose to ignore it because it proves convenient to do so.'[12] The privileged sleepwalk and let the unjust world order go on unchecked. Perhaps this is why Jesus said, 'Again I tell you, it is easier for a camel to go through the eye of a needle than for someone who is rich to enter the kingdom of God' (Matt. 19:24). (Incidentally, Aramaic-speaking scholars translate the original term as rope rather than camel. Since Jesus was also an Aramaic-speaking person, there is good reason to believe that this is the correct translation.[13])

Jesus, who said 'But woe to you who are rich' (Luke 6:24), also said 'Blessed are you who are poor, for yours is the kingdom of God' (Luke 6:20). Injustice causes constant pain to the *anawim*, the poor of Yahweh. One who is comfortable sleeps; one in constant pain does not. A person who is awake can stand against unjust social orders, while a sleepwalker cannot. 'Who are better prepared than the oppressed to understand the terrible significance of an oppressive society? Who suffer the effects of oppression more than the oppressed? Who can better understand the necessity of liberation?'[14]

The oppressed groups might understand the necessity of liberation, but what means would they adopt? In today's world some groups have chosen violent means. One week after the 11 September 2001 (when the terrorists struck New York and the World Trade Center fell), Suheir Hammad, a Palestinian woman brought up in New York, wrote:

> I do not know how bad a life has to break in order to kill.
> I have never been so hungry that I willed hunger.
> I have never been so angry as to want to control a gun over
>   a pen.
> Not really. Even as a woman, as a Palestinian, as a broken
>   human being.
> Never this broken.[15]

When oppressed groups suffer they try to destroy the oppressors who perpetuate injustice. They strike. The attacked group then mirrors the same evil and hits back. This creates a never-ending cycle of violence.

Violence is a human instinct, but not the only one. Walter Wink observes: 'Human evolution has provided the species with two deeply instinctual responses to violence: flight or fight.'[16] He uses the term fight here to mean violent fight. While the western Christian governments often choose the second option of fighting violently, ordinary church members adopt the first option: flight. In response to the continuing injustice of racism church people still tend to look or turn away. I agree with Wink when he claims that both responses – flight and violent fight – are contrary to gospel values. Jesus offers a third way: non-violent direct action.[17] I understand that instinctual responses are the values of the kingdom of the world. Jesus brought about the Kingdom of God in which human beings transform their fighting instinct and instead of breaking each other they build each other up. They also win over their instinct to run away, to keep quiet about injustice. Martin Luther King knew well about the sin of silence. 'We will have to repent,' he said, 'not merely for the vitriolic words and actions of the bad people but for the appalling silence of the good people.'[18] Silence is a collusive cover-up.

Jesus was an exemplary missionary, always moving from the margin to the centre and back again. He had one foot in the establishment and one foot on the edge of society. People who have access to both the centre and the margin usually bring about change. Black Anglicans, being the 'house Negroes', are perfectly placed. They can never be too comfortable in the comfort zone, so they challenge the house. Moreover, they can challenge it because they are already in it. The stories in the book affirm that Black Anglicans have risen above their instinctual responses. They have not preferred the gun to the pen. They have not been violent, neither have they remained silent.

Malcolm X was worried that since the 'house Negroes' were too close to the slave masters, they would love the master too much and validate their own oppression. However, love is the first criterion for resisting what is evil. We do not repay anyone evil for evil (Rom. 12:17, 21; 1 Thess. 5:15; 1 Pet. 3:9). If because of our skin colour the image of God in us is disregarded, instead of mirroring that – instead of disregarding God's image in White people – we insist that we are created in God's image as much as they are. We might be hated for our skin colour, but we refuse to hate the white skin colour. We hate racism, but not White people. We want to join in with James Baldwin and say courageously:

> Everything now, we must assume, is in our hands; we have no right to assume otherwise. If we – and now I mean the relatively conscious whites and the relatively conscious blacks, who must like lovers, insist on, or create, the consciousness of the others – do not falter in our duty now, we may be able, handful that we are, to end the racial nightmare, and achieve our country, and change the history of the world.[19]

Some of the things the Black Anglicans have done match with a chart presented by Wink under the heading 'Jesus' Third Way':

+ Seize the moral initiative.
+ Find a creative alternative to violence.
+ Assert your own humanity and dignity as a person.
+ Meet force with ridicule or humour.
+ Break the cycle of humiliation.
+ Refuse to submit to or to accept the inferior position.
+ Expose the injustice of the system.
+ Take control of the power dynamic.
+ Shame the oppressor into repentance.
+ Stand your ground.
+ Make the powers make decisions for which they are not prepared.
+ Recognize your own power.
+ Be willing to suffer rather than retaliate.
+ Force the oppressor to see you in a new light.
+ Deprive the oppressor of a situation where a show of force is effective.
+ Be willing to undergo the penalty of breaking unjust laws.
+ Die to fear of the old order and its rules.
+ Seek the oppressor's transformation.[20]

While the West is individualistic, non-western cultures believe in mutuality. Here again Black Anglicans are in a good position to end racism. Black and White people are in an unavoidable network of interdependence. If racism tries to destroy Black humanity, it invariably damages White humanity.

> We are caught in an inescapable network of mutuality, tied to a single garment of destiny. What affects one directly, affects all

indirectly. As long as there is poverty in this world, [no one] can be totally healthy ... Strangely enough, I can never be what I ought to be until you are what you ought to be. You can never be what you ought to be until I am what I ought to be.[21]

The Black Anglicans who have experienced something of the joy of resurrection know that resurrection is not an individualistic privilege for one to hold selfishly. Many Eastern Orthodox icons depict the risen Christ breaking the gates of the underworld with tremendous force, entering into it to grab hold of the wrists of Adam and Eve to pull them out. According to these icons Jesus did not rise alone; with him Adam and Eve, meaning the whole of humanity, rose again. These icons are based on biblical passages such as Matthew 16:18 and 27:52–54.

Just as stories of rejection and of resistance constitute a challenge to the whole of the Church of England, so tales of resurrection are a source of encouragement and hope, shared with the whole Church. In this book testimony has been given to the many ways in which the Spirit of the Risen Christ continues to inspire and renew the lives of the people of God. Black and Asian people have testified to the support they have received from their own families, communities and congregations; they have told of the difference made when White people have responded to the call of their sisters and brothers; and they have shown how the truth of the gospel has been the more clearly proclaimed through the growing together in the Church of people of very different cultures and histories.

In telling their stories Black and Asian Anglicans have opened their resurrected wounds and have invited their readers saying, 'Come see, come touch; don't run away from the pain; see if you too can know something of the joy of resurrection.' As readers touch the wounds they might feel moved, emotionally touched, and say,

> Who touched me? Somebody touched me
> And I pray
> Stay with us, Lord, as we work for a better world.[22]

Notes

Introduction

1. Author unknown, 'A Psalm for All Who Keep God's Word', in Hai Ok Hwang and Binh Nguyen OP, 'Gathering ceremony' in *In God's Image*, vol. 16, no. 4 (Kuala Lumpur, Asian Women's Resource Centre for Culture and Theology, 1997), pp. 10–11.
2. Chung Hyun Kyung, *Struggle to be the Sun Again: Introducing Asian Women's Theology* (London, SCM Press, 1991), p. 104. She used these words regarding Asian women's stories.
3. James H. Cone, *God of the Oppressed* (San Francisco, Harper & Row, 1975), p. 16.
4. *Kairos* is a New Testament Greek word. The decisive epoch waited for is one of its meaning. See *kairos* in the Lexicon. Available from http://www.crosswalk.com (accessed 10 March 2005).
5. Barbara Findlay, *With All of Who We are: A Discussion of Oppression and Dominance* (Vancouver, Lazara Press, 1991), p. 12.
6. David Haslam, *Race for the Millennium: A Challenge to Church and Society* (London, Church House Publishing, 1996), p. 9.
7. Judy Pearsall (ed.), *The New Oxford Dictionary of English* (Oxford, Clarendon Press, 1998), p. 1526. Race: 'Origin early 16th cent. (denoting a group with common features): via French from Italian *razza*, of unknown ultimate origin.'
8. Emmanuel Chukwudi Eze (ed.), *Race and Enlightenment: A Reader* (Oxford, Blackwell, 1997), p. 5.
9. ibid., see pp. 13–14, 41–2, 48, 84–90 and 104–8.
10. Peter Fryer, *Staying Power: The History of Black People in Britain* (London, Pluto Press, 1984), p. 133.
11. ibid., p. 167.
12. See under 'Caucasian' in Pearsall (ed.), *Dictionary*, p. 290.
13. See Eze (ed.), *Race*, pp. 84–5. See also Pearsall (ed.), *Dictionary*, p. 290.
14. Tony Kelly, 'The Bail Race is a Rat Race Not Fit for the Human Race', a masters degree dissertation in Socio-legal Studies (Birmingham, Birmingham University, 1991), p. 5.
15. John. L. Wilkinson, *The Church in Black and White* (Edinburgh, St Andrew, 1993), p. 23.
16. Robert Beckford, *Jesus is Dread* (London, Darton, Longman & Todd, 1998), pp. 44 and 48.
17. 'Symbols of Hate'. Available from http://gbgm-umc.org/umw/anti-hate/symbolsofhate.html (accessed 4 March 2005).
18. Unless otherwise stated, all biblical references are to the New Revised Standard Version with Apocrypha (NRSV).
19. Beckford, *Jesus*, p. 48.

20. Haslam, *Race for the Millenium*, pp. 12–13.
21. See under 'White' in Pearsall (ed.), *Dictionary*, p. 2105.
22. Abby L. Ferber, 'What White supremacists taught a Jewish scholar about identity' in Margaret L. Anderson and Patricia Hill Collins (eds.), *Race, Class and Gender: An Anthology* (London, International Thomson Publishing Europe, 1998), p. 117.
23. Gen Doy, *Black Visual Culture: Modernity and Postmodernity* (London and New York, I. B. Tauris and Co. Ltd, 2000), p. 9.
24. Kelly Brown Douglas, *The Black Christ* (Maryknoll, NY, Orbis Books, 1994), p. 35.
25. Fryer, *Staying Power*, p. 1.
26. Hilary Beckles, 'Columbus and the contemporary dispensation within the Caribbean' in Paul Grant and Raj Patel (eds.), *A Time to Act* (Birmingham, Racial Justice and The Black and Third World Theological Working Group, 1992), p. 43.
27. Emmanuel Y. Lartey, *In Living Colour: An Intercultural Approach to Pastoral Care and Counselling* (London, Cassell, 1997), p. 98.
28. James H. Cone, *A Black Theology of Liberation*, 20th anniversary edn (Maryknoll, NY, Orbis Books, 1990), p. v.
29. Anthony G. Reddie, *Faith Stories and the Experience of Black Elders: Singing the Lord's Song in a Strange Land* (London, Jessica Kingsley Publishers, 2001), p. 117.
30. Desmond Tutu in Tracy Sukraw, 'Desmond Tutu says racism is the "ultimate blasphemy"'. Available from http://www.episcopalchurch.org/3577_20571_ENG_HTM.htm (accessed 30 September 2004).
31. ibid.
32. 'By his wounds you have been healed' in Iben Gjerding and Katherine Kinnamon (eds.), *No Longer Strangers: A Resource for Women and Worship* (Geneva, WCC Publications, 1983), p. 33.
33. Tutu in Sukraw, 'Desmond Tutu'.

1   Motherland, Here I Come

1. © Vilma Jarrett-Harvey, 'Mother Land', 2004.
2. Peter Fryer, *Staying Power: The History of Black People in Britain* (London, Pluto Press, 1984), p 373.
3. M. Manley, *History of West Indies Cricket* (London, Deutsch, 1988), p. 123, cited in Peter L. Edmead, *The Divisive Decade: A History of Caribbean Immigration to Birmingham in the 1950s* (Birmingham, Birmingham Library Services, 1999), p. 28.
4. Edmead, *Divisive Decade*, p. 28.
5. James H. Cone, *God of the Oppressed* (San Francisco, Harper & Row, 1975), pp. 17 and 21.
6. Fryer, *Staying Power*, p. 374.
7. Maya Angelou, on the radio.
8. Barbara Findlay, *With All of Who We Are: A Discussion of Oppression and Dominance* (Vancouver, Lazara Press, 1991), p. 6.
9. David Haslam, *The Churches and 'Race': A Pastoral Approach* (Cambridge, Grove Books Limited, 2001), p. 23.

2 Clinging to the Future

1. © Janet Johnson, 'The Reason Why', part 2, 2004.
2. Prayers of Penitence in Holy Communion in *Common Worship: Services and Prayers for the Church of England* (London, Archbishops' Council, 2000).
3. Barbara Findlay, *With All of Who We Are: A Discussion of Oppression and Dominance* (Vancouver, Lazara Press, 1991), p. 6.
4. John. L. Wilkinson, *The Church in Black and White* (Edinburgh, St Andrew, 1993), p. 174.
5. Peter Fryer, *Staying Power: The History of Black People in Britain* (London, Pluto Press, 1984), p. 144.
6. ibid., p. 169.
7. ibid., p. 149.
8. ibid., p. 169.
9. Sir William Macpherson, *The Stephen Lawrence Enquiry Report* (London, The Stationery Office, 1999), ch. 6.17.
10. Peggy McIntosh, 'White privilege and male privilege: a personal account of coming to see correspondences through work in Women's Studies' in Margaret L. Anderson and Patricia Hill Collins (eds.), *Race, Class and Gender: An Anthology* (London, International Thomson Publishing Europe, 1998), p. 102.
11. Haslam, *Churches and 'Race'*, p. 19.
12. Delores S. Williams, *Sisters in the Wilderness: The Challenge of Womanist God-Talk* (Maryknoll, NY, Orbis Books, 1993), p. 199.
13. James H. Cone, *A Black Theology of Liberation*, 20th anniversary edn (Maryknoll, NY, Orbis Books, 1990), p. 16.
14. ibid., p. 20.
15. See Mukti Barton, *Scripture as Empowerment for Liberation and Justice: The Experience of Christian and Muslim Women in Bangladesh* (Bristol, University of Bristol, 1999), pp. 102–4 and Williams, *Sisters*, pp. 196–9.

3 Communion! What Communion?

1. © Vilma Jarrett-Harvey, 'Rejection, Resistance and Resurrection', 2004.
2. J. Grenville, *The Collins History of the World in the Twentieth Century* (London, Harper Collins, 1994), p. 504, cited in Peter L. Edmead, *The Divisive Decade: A History of Caribbean Immigration to Birmingham in the 1950s* (Birmingham, Birmingham Library Services, 1999), p. 9.
3. A description of Fertile Crescent. Available from http://www.geocities.com/CapitolHill/Parliament/2587/fc.html (accessed 24 March 2005).
4. Clarice J. Martin, 'A chamberlain's journey and the challenge of interpretation for liberation' in Norman K. Gottwald and Richard A. Horsley (eds.), *The Bible and Liberation: Political and Social Hermeneutics* (Maryknoll, NY, Orbis Books; London, SPCK, 1993), p. 488.
5. Cain Hope Felder (ed.), *The Original African Heritage Study Bible* (Tennessee, The James C. Winston Publishing Company, 1993), p. 94.
6. ibid., p. xi.
7. ibid., p. 102.
8. 'Voices from the crowd: Holy Week meditation' in Wild Goose Worship Group, *Stages on the Way: Worship Resources for Lent, Holy Week and Easter* (Glasgow, Wild Goose Publications, 1998), p. 150.
9. Renita J. Weems, 'Womanist reflections on biblical hermeneutics' in James H.

Cone and Gayraud S. Wilmore (eds.), *Black Theology, a Documentary History*, vol. 2 (Maryknoll, NY, Orbis Books, 1993), p. 216.

10. For the term 'Nigger', see Judy Pearsall (ed.), *The New Oxford Dictionary of English* (Oxford, Clarendon Press, 1998), p. 1252.

4 Still I Rise

1. © Vilma Jarrett-Harvey, 'Still I Rise', 2004.
2. Some biblical verses regarding the strangers: Exod. 12:49; Exod. 22:21–24; Exod. 23:9; Lev. 19:10, 33, 34; Lev. 23:22; Lev. 24:22; Num. 15:15, 16, 29; Deut. 1:16; Deut. 10:18; Deut. 23:7; Deut. 24:14, 17, 19, 20–21; Deut. 26:12–13; Deut. 27:19; Ps. 94:6–10; Ps. 146:9; Jer. 7:6; Jer. 22:3; Ezek. 22:7, 29; Ezek. 47:23; Zech. 7:10; Mal. 3:5.
3. Kahlil Gibran, *The Prophet* (London, Heinemann, 1974), p. 36.
4. John. L. Wilkinson, *The Church in Black and White* (Edinburgh, St Andrew, 1993), p. 33.
5. John Allen, *The Essential Desmond Tutu*, Mayibuye History and Literature Series no. 85 (Cape Town, David Phillip and University of the Western Cape), 1997, pp. 8–9, in *Called to Act Justly: A Challenge to Include Minority Ethnic People in the Life of the Church of England* (London, Archbishop's Council, 2003), p. 6.
6. ibid., p. 6.
7. Paulo Freire, *Pedagogy of Hope: Reliving Pedagogy of the Oppressed*, trans. Robert R. Barr (New York, Continuum, 1994), p. 46.
8. ibid., p. 46.
9. Paulo Freire, *Pedagogy of the Oppressed*, trans. Myra Bergman Ramos, (London, Penguin Books, 1996), p. 46.
10. Bob Marley, 'Redemption Song' in Nick Crispin (comp.), *Bob Marley: The Chord Songbook* (London, Wise Publications, 1999), pp. 36–7.
11. Cecil Cone, *The Identity Crisis in Black Theology* (Nashville, AMEC, 1975), p. 37, cited in Kelly Brown Douglas, *The Black Christ* (Maryknoll, NY, Orbis Books, 1994), p. 21.
12. Brown Douglas, *Black Christ*, p. 25.
13. ibid., pp. 17–27.

5 To Be Free or Not To Be Free

1. © Janet Johnson, 'Contemporary Vibes', adapted from William Shakespeare's *Hamlet*, 2004.
2. Peter Brierley, *The Tide is Running Out: What the English Church Survey Reveals* (London, Christian Research, 2000), p. 136.
3. *The Giles Fraser Column*, 'Imperial Christianity', 6 October 2003. Available from http://www.ekklesia.co.uk (accessed 19 October 2004).
4. Brierley, *Tide*, p. 140.
5. Ivor Smith-Cameron, *The Church of Many Colours* (London, Ivor Smith-Cameron, 1998), p. 288.
6. Lorraine Dixon, 'A reflection on Black identity and belonging in the context of the Anglican Church in England: a way forward', *Black Theology in Britain: A Journal of Contextual Praxis*, issue 4 (Sheffield, Sheffield Academic Press Ltd., 2000), p. 30.
7. For a contextual reading of the Samaritan woman's story see Mukti Barton, *Scripture as Empowerment for Liberation and Justice: The Experience of Christian*

and Muslim Women in Bangladesh (Bristol, University of Bristol, 1999), pp. 107–18.

8. Smith-Cameron, *Church of Many Colours*, op. cit., pp. 141–2.
9. Now Smitha Prasadam is ordained and will be mentioned again in Chapter 7.
10. The Archbishop's Council's Committee for Minority Ethnic Anglican Concerns, *Serving God in Church and Community: Vocations for Minority Ethnic Anglicans in the Church of England* (London, Church House Publishing, 2000), p. 24.
11. ibid., p. 26.
12. Birmingham diocesan database, 2004.
13. 2001 Census. Available from http://www.birmingham.gov.uk/ GenerateContent?CONTENT_ITEM_ID=26205&CONTENT_ITEM_TYPE=0 &MENU_ID=12672&EXPAND=11333 (accessed 18 February 2005).
14. Brierley, *Tide*, p. 134.
15. 'Negro Spirituals: Songs of Survival'. Available from http://www. jsfmusic.com/Uncle_Tom/Tom_Article3.html (accessed 28 October 2004).

6   Refusing To Be Invisible

1. Adapted from Kasimbayan, 'Untitled' in Sharon Rose Joy Ruiz-Duremded (ed.), *Unleashing the Power Within Us, Meditations for Asian Women* (Quezon City, National Council of Churches in the Philippines, 2001), p. 81.
2. Ivor Smith-Cameron, *The Church of Many Colours* (London, Ivor Smith-Cameron, 1998), p. 251.
3. ibid., p. 139.
4. Stephen Gill, 'About the author' in Peter C. Mall, *Hamd-O-Sana* (Jalandhar, Peter's Publication, 1999).
5. ibid.
6. For the life of Sadhu Sundar Singh, see C. F. Andrews, *Sadhu Sundar Singh: A Personal Memoir* (London, Hodder & Stoughton, 1937); and A. J. Appasamy, *Sadhu Sundar Singh: A Biography* (Madras, The Christian Literature Society, 1966).
7. Sarfraz Manzoor, *Don't Call Me Asian*. Available from http://www. dawn.com/2005/01/12/int14.htm (accessed 8 February 2005).
8. Bhikhu Parekh, *et al.*, *The Future of Multi-Ethnic Britain: The Parekh Report* (London, Runnymede Trust, 2000), p. 27.

7   The Truth Sets Us Free

1. © Janet Johnson, 'What is Truth?', 1998.
2. Eve Pitts, 'Black Womanist Ethic' in Paul Grant and Raj Patel (eds.), *A Time to Speak* (Birmingham, Racial Justice and Black Theology Working Group, 1991), p. 33.
3. Bhikhu Parekh, *et al.*, *The Future of Multi-Ethnic Britain: The Parekh Report* (London, Runnymede Trust, 2000), p. 65.
4. 'Religion in India: Christianity', September 1995. Available from http://atheism.about.com/library/world/AJ/bl_IndiaOtherChristianity.htm (accessed 29 June 2004).
5. 'Early Christianity in Britain'. Available from http://www.britainexpress. com/History/Early_Christian_Britain.htm (accessed 29 June 2004).
6. William Dalrymple, 'The incredible journey: did St Thomas found a church

in South India? William Dalrymple unravels a Christian mystery' in Saturday Review, *Guardian*, 15 April 2000.

7. ibid.

8. *Acts of the Holy Apostle Thomas*. Available from http://www.ccel.org/fathers2/ANF-08/anf08-99.htm (accessed 23 February 2005).

9. T. V. Philip, 'East of the Euphrates: Early Christianity in Asia'. Available from http://www.religiononline.org/showchapter.asp?title=1553&C=1364 (accessed 23 February 2005).

10. 'Apostle St Thomas in India'. Available from http://members.tripod.com/~Berchmans/apostle.html and http://www.indianchristianity.org/thomas.html (accessed 22 February 2005).

11. 'Religion in Britain, and in the Rest of the UK'. Available from http://www.religioustolerance.org/uk_rel.htm (accessed 11 July 2004).

12. 'Religion in India: Christianity': see note 4.

13. Stephen B. Bevans, *Models of Contextual Theology* (Maryknoll, NY, Orbis Books, 1992), p. 7.

14. 'Diversity, Social Cohesion and Opportunity: The Asian Example'. Available from http://www.article13.com/A13_ContentList.asp?strAction=Get Publication&PNID=640 as retrieved on 27 October 2004 10:08:41 GMT (accessed 10 November 2004).

15. Parekh, *Future*, p. 28.

16. Raj Patel, 'Why do Christians wear ties?' in Paul Grant and Raj Patel (eds.), *A Time to Speak* (Birmingham, Racial Justice and Black Theology Working Group, 1991), p. 87.

8   Stand Up for What Is Right

1. © Janet Johnson, 'Sometimes Saying "I'm Sorry" Is not Enough: A Tribute to Stephen Lawrence', 1998.

2. Paulo Freire, *Pedagogy of the Oppressed*, trans. Myra Bergman Ramos, (London, Penguin Books, 1996), pp. 68–9.

3. *Seeds of Hope: Building a Black, Asian and White Church* (Birmingham, The Diocese of Birmingham, 1999). The Birmingham study pack drew on what had been prepared for the Church of England as a whole by its Committee for Minority Ethnic Anglican Concerns. *Seeds of Hope* was launched in September 1999 by Bishop Mark Santer, the Bishop of Birmingham at that time. All the parishes were urged to study the course within a period of three years.

4. Matthew, cited in Maurice Hobbs, *Better Will Come: A Pastoral Response to Institutional Racism in British Churches* (Nottingham, Grove Books, 1991), p. 5.

5. Jean-Paul Sartre, 'Preface' in Frantz Fanon, *The Wretched of the Earth*, trans. Constance Farrington (London, Penguin Books, 1967), p. 23.

6. Audre Lorde, *Sister Outsider: Essays and Speeches* (Freedom, CA, Crossing, 1984), p. 130.

7. Paul Grant, 'If it happened to you, tell me what would you do?' in Paul Grant and Raj Patel (eds.), *A Time to Speak* (Birmingham, Racial Justice and Black Theology Working Group, 1991), p. 52.

8. 'Government and police must engage communities to build a fairer criminal justice system'. Available from http://www.homeoffice.gov.uk/n_story.asp?item_id=991 (accessed 17 November 2004).

9. Barbara Findlay, *With All of Who We Are: A Discussion of Oppression and Dominance* (Vancouver, Lazara Press, 1991), p. 6.
10. Robert Beckford, *Jesus is Dread* (London, Darton, Longman & Todd, 1998), p. 56.
11. Here the reference is from *Good News Bible with Apocrypha/Deuterocanonical Books* (Glasgow, HarperCollins, 1993).
12. Beckford, *Jesus*, pp. 12–13.
13. Desmond Tutu, *Hope and Suffering* (London, Fount Paperbacks, 1984), p. 18.
14. Here the reference is from *Good News Bible*.

9   Paving the Way

1. © Janet Johnson, 'African Queens', 1998.
2. A. Clutton-Brock, 'The English Bible' in V. F. Storr (ed.), *The English Bible: Essays by Various Authors* (London, Methuen & Co. Ltd., 1938), p. 78, cited in R. S. Sugirtharajah, *Postcolonial Criticism and Biblical Interpretation* (Oxford, Oxford University Press, 2002), p. 128.
3. Sugirtharajah, *Postcolonial Criticism*, pp. 128–9.
4. ibid., pp. 146 and 148.
5. *The Holy Bible, Authorised King James Version* (London, William Collins Sons & Co. Ltd., 1954).
6. Piero della Francesca (1416–92), 'Annunciation', a fresco, in *The Holy Bible, Authorised King James Version*, colour plate no. xx.
7. See Exod. 20:4–5; Lev. 19:4; Lev. 26:1; Deut. 4:23, 25; Deut. 7:25; Deut. 12:3; Ps 97:7 and Rom. 1:23.
8. Kate Coleman, 'Black Theology and Black Liberation: A Womanist Perspective', *Black Theology in Britain: A Journal of Contextual Praxis*, issue 1 (Sheffield, Sheffield Academic Press, 1998), pp. 62–3.
9. Cain Hope Felder (ed.), *The Original African Heritage Study Bible* (Tennessee, The James C. Winston Publishing Company, 1993), p. 95.
10. ibid., p. 96.
11. Christopher Kelly, 'Gibson goes for shock value over substance' in Fort Worth Star-Telegram. Available from http://www.philly.com/mld/philly/entertainment/special_packages/passion_of_christ/8028323.htm?1c (accessed 24 February 2005).
12. Hisako Kinukawa, 'The Syrophoenician Woman: Mark 7.24–30' in R. S. Sugirtharajah, *Voices from the Margin: Interpreting the Bible in the Third World*, revised edn (London, SPCK, 1995), p. 149.
13. Clarence H. Wagner, Jr, 'Commerce in the Bible, Israel - Crossroads of the East'. Available from http://www.bridgesforpeace.com/publications/dispatch/everydaylife/Article-28.html (accessed 21 January 2005).
14. Gay L. Byron, *Symbolic Blackness and Ethnic Difference in Early Christian Literature* (London and New York, Routledge, 2002), p. 4.
15. Glenn Usry and Craig S. Keener, *Black Man's Religion: Can Christianity be Afrocentric?* (Illinois, Inter Varsity Press, 1996), pp. 75–6.
16. ibid., p. 52.
17. Emmanuel Chukwudi Eze (ed.), *Race and Enlightenment: A Reader* (Oxford, Blackwell, 1997), p. 33.
18. ibid., p. 63.
19. Robin DiAngelo, 'Heterosexism: addressing internalized dominance', *Journal of Progressive Human Services*, vol. 8, no. 1 (1997), pp. 13–14.

20. Peggy McIntosh, 'White privilege and male privilege: a personal account of coming to see correspondences through work in Women's Studies' in Margaret L. Anderson and Patricia Hill Collins (eds.), *Race, Class and Gender: An Anthology* (London, International Thomson Publishing Europe, 1998), p. 102.
21. ibid., p. 102.

10   The Proud Black Sheep of the Family

1. © Janet Johnson, 'To be Black is Beautiful', 1998.
2. 'N-G-R, niger, negro "nigger": the n word from divine to racist'. Available from http://community2.webtv.net/PAULNUBIAEMPIRE/TRACKING AND/ (accessed 20 October 2004).
3. Robert B. Moore, 'Racist stereotyping in the English language' in Margaret L. Anderson and Patricia Hill Collins (eds.), *Race, Class and Gender: An Anthology* (London, International Thomson Publishing Europe, 1998), p. 332. 'The Environment of Language', editorial, *Saturday Review*, 8 April 1967, cited in Moore.
4. David Haslam, *The Churches and 'Race': A Pastoral Approach* (Cambridge, Grove Books Limited, 2001), p. 21.
5. Moore, 'Racist stereotyping', p. 332.
6. Judy Pearsall (ed.), *The New Oxford Dictionary of English* (Oxford, Clarendon Press, 1998), p. 1435.
7. See above note 5.
8. *Seeds of Hope: Building a Black, Asian and White Church* (Birmingham, The Diocese of Birmingham, 1999). When the course was reviewed this was a comment from a Black Anglican congregation.
9. Pearsall, *Dictionary*, pp. 180–3.
10. ibid., pp. 2105–7.
11. See note 3.
12. Chung Hyun Kyung, '"Han-pu-ri": Doing Theology from Korean Women's Perspective' in Virginia Fabella and Sun Ai Lee Park (eds.), *We Dare to Dream: Doing Theology as Asian Women* (Maryknoll, NY, Orbis Books, 1990), p. 138.
13. For colour terms in the Bible, see Mukti Barton, 'I am Black and beautiful', *Black Theology: An International Journal*, vol. 2, no. 2 (London, Equinox Publishing Ltd, 2004), pp. 167–87.

11   God's Community of Resistance

1. © Sharon Palmer, 'The Reality of Crime', 1995.
2. National Statistics: News Release. Available from http://www.statistics.gov.uk/pdfdir/migr1104.pdf (accessed 23 November 2004).
3. Bhikhu Parekh, *et al.*, *The Future of Multi-Ethnic Britain: The Parekh Report* (London, Runnymede Trust, 2000), p. 63.
4. Inderjit Bhogal, 'Mind your language', *Methodist Recorder*, 15 February 2001.
5. Robert Beckford, *Jesus is Dread* (London, Darton, Longman & Todd, 1998), p. 26.
6. Who are Free Methodists? Available from http://www.freemethodist church.org/Sections/About%20Us/Basic%20Info/FAQs/What's%20A%20 Free%20Methodist.htm (accessed 11 November 2004).
7. Elsa Tamez, 'The scandalous message of James: the angle of praxis' in Norman K. Gottwald and Richard A. Horsley (eds.), *The Bible and Liberation:*

Political and Social Hermeneutics (Maryknoll, NY, Orbis Books; London, SPCK, 1993), p. 532.

8. James H. Cone, 'Theology's great sin: silence in the face of White supremacy', *Black Theology: An International Journal*, vol. 2, no. 2 (London, Equinox Publishing Ltd, July 2004), p. 142.

9. Joshua Gee, *The Trade and Navigation of Great-Britain Considered* (Sam. Buckley, 1729), pp. 25, 126, in Fryer, op. cit., p. 17.

10. Peter Fryer, *Staying Power: The History of Black People in Britain* (London, Pluto Press, 1984), p. 16.

11. Cone, 'Theology's great sin', p. 146.

12. James H. Cone, *A Black Theology of Liberation*, 20th anniversary edn (Maryknoll, NY, Orbis Books, 1990), p. 70.

13. For a full discussion on these passages see Walter Wink, *Engaging the Powers* (Minneapolis, Fortress Press, 1992), pp. 175–93.

14. Stanley Cohen, *States of Denial: Knowing about Atrocities and Suffering* (Cambridge, Polity Press, 2001), pp. 119, 131 and 133.

15. Judy Pearsall (ed.), *The New Oxford Dictionary of English* (Oxford, Clarendon Press, 1998), pp. 362–3.

16. Paul Grant, 'If it happened to you, tell me what would you do?' in Paul Grant and Raj Patel (eds.), *A Time to Speak* (Birmingham, Racial Justice and Black Theology Working Group, 1991), p. 48.

17. Beckford, *Jesus*, p. 31.

12   Watching You

1. Nicola Slee, 'Veneration of the Cross' in Nicola Slee, *Praying Like a Woman* (London, SPCK, 2004), p. 38.

2. George Orwell, *Nineteen-Eighty Four* (Harmondsworth, Penguin, 1954; first pub. 1949), p. 31.

3. *Insight Guide: The Dominican Republic and Haiti* (Singapore Branch, Apa Publications Gmbh & Co. Verlag KG, 2000), p. 31.

4. Hilary Beckles, 'Columbus and the contemporary dispensation within the Caribbean' in Paul Grant and Raj Patel (eds.), *A Time to Act* (Birmingham, Racial Justice and The Black and Third World Theological Working Group, 1992), p. 44.

5. Peter Fryer, *Staying Power: The History of Black People in Britain* (London, Pluto Press, 1984), pp. 179–80.

6. ibid., p. 181.

7. Howard Zinn, *Columbus and Western Civilization*. Available from http://www.geocities.com/howardzinnfans/CDay.html (accessed 2 February 2005).

8. ibid.

9. Beckels, in Grant and Patel (eds.), *Time to Act*, p. 44.

10. James Baldwin, 'Stranger in the Village' in Henry Louis Gates, Jr and Neille Y. McKay (eds.), *The Norton Anthology: African American Literature* (New York and London, W. W. Norton & Company, 1997), p. 1674.

11. Frantz Fanon, *The Wretched of the Earth*, trans. Constance Farrington (London, Penguin Books, 1967), p. 84.

12. Frantz Fanon, *Black Skin, White Masks*, trans. Charles Lam Markmann (London, Pluto Press, 1986), p. 139.

13. Mary Keller, 'Raced and gendered perspectives: towards the epidermaliza-

tion of subjectivity in Religious Studies theory' in Ursula King and Tina Beattie (eds.), *Gender, Religion and Diversity, Cross-Cultural Perspectives* (London and New York, Continuum, 2004), p. 84.

14. Pete Ward, *Youthwork and the Mission of God, Frameworks for Relational Outreach* (London, SPCK, 1997), pp. 83–4.

Conclusion

1. Linda Jones/CAFOD, 'A Healing Touch'.
2. Robert Beckford, *Jesus is Dread* (London, Darton, Longman & Todd, 1998), pp. 42–58.
3. John Bright, *A History of Israel* (London, SCM Press, 1972), pp. 93–4. See also Cyris H. S. Moon, 'A Korean minjung perspective: the Hebrews and the Exodus' in R. S. Sugirtharajah (ed.), *Voices from the Margin* (London, SPCK, 1991), p. 242.
4. Julio De Santa Ana, *Good News to the Poor: The Challenge of the Poor in the History of the Church* (Madras, The Christian Literature Society, 1978), p. 9.
5. Judy Pearsall (ed.), *The New Oxford Dictionary of English* (Oxford, Clarendon Press, 1998), pp. 510–11. Septuagint is a Greek Version of the Hebrew Bible.
6. ibid., pp. 510–11.
7. Peggy McIntosh, 'White privilege and male privilege: a personal account of coming to see correspondences through work in Women's Studies' in Margaret L. Anderson and Patricia Hill Collins (eds.), *Race, Class and Gender: An Anthology* (London, International Thomson Publishing Europe, 1998), p. 95.
8. ibid., pp. 97–100.
9. Barbara Findlay, *With All of Who We Are: A Discussion of Oppression and Dominance* (Vancouver, Lazara Press, 1991), p. 5.
10. ibid., p. 5.
11. See Introduction note 6.
12. Stanley Cohen, *States of Denial: Knowing about Atrocities and Suffering* (Cambridge, Polity Press, 2001), pp. 33 and 80.
13. See Matthew 19:24 in George M. Lamsa, *Holy Bible from the Ancient Eastern Text: George M. Lamsa's Translation From the Aramaic of the Peshitta* (New York, Harper Collins Publishers, 1968).
14. Paulo Freire, *Pedagogy of the Oppressed*, trans. Myra Bergman Ramos, (London, Penguin Books, 1996), p. 27.
15. Suheir Hammad, cited in Rowan Williams, *Writing in the Dust: Reflections on 11th September and its Aftermath* (London, Hodder & Stoughton, 2002), p. 18.
16. Walter Wink, *Engaging the Powers* (Minneapolis, Fortress Press, 1992), p. 175.
17. ibid., p. 175.
18. Martin Luther King, Jr, 'Letter from Birmingham City Jail' in James M. Washington (ed.), *A Testament of Hope: The Essential Writings of Martin Luther King, Jr.* (San Francisco, Harper & Row, 1986), p. 296, cited in James H. Cone, 'Theology's great sin: silence in the face of White supremacy', *Black Theology: An International Journal*, vol. 2, no. 2 (London, Equinox Publishing Ltd, July 2004), p. 139.
19. James Baldwin, *The Fire Next Time* (London, Penguin, 1964), p. 89.
20. Wink, *Engaging the Powers*, pp. 186–7.
21. Martin Luther King, Jr, 'The American Dream', *Negro History Bulletin*, vol. 31,

(May 1968), p. 12, cited in James H. Cone, *Black Theology of Liberation*, 20th anniversary edn (Maryknoll, NY, Orbis Books, 1990) , p. xvii.
22. See note 1.

Bibliography

Allen, John, *The Essential Desmond Tutu*, Mayibuye History and Literature Series no. 85 (Cape Town, David Phillip and University of the Western Cape, 1997), pp. 8–9 in *Called to Act Justly: A Challenge to Include Minority Ethnic People in the Life of the Church of England* (London, The Archbishops' Council, 2003).

Anderson, Margaret L. and Hill Collins, Patricia (eds.), *Race, Class and Gender: An Anthology* (London, International Thomson Publishing Europe, 1998).

Andrews, C. F., *Sadhu Sundar Singh: A Personal Memoir* (London, Hodder & Stoughton, 1937).

Appasamy, A. J., *Sadhu Sundar Singh: A Biography* (Madras, The Christian Literature Society, 1966).

Archbishops' Council, *Common Worship: Services and Prayers for the Church of England* (London, The Archbishops' Council, 2000).

Archbishops' Council's Committee for Minority Ethnic Anglican Concerns, *Serving God in Church and Community: Vocations for Minority Ethnic Anglicans in the Church of England* (London, Church House Publishing, 2000).

Archbishops' Council, *Called to Act Justly: A Challenge to Include Minority Ethnic People in the Life of the Church of England* (London, The Archbishop's Council, 2003).

Author unknown, 'A Psalm for All Who Keep God's Word' in Hai Ok Hwang and Binh Nguyen OP, 'Gathering ceremony', *In God's Image*, vol. 16, no. 4 (Kuala Lumpur, Asian Women's Resource Centre for Culture and Theology, 1997).

Baldwin, James, 'Stranger in the village' in Henry Louis Gates, Jr and Neille Y. McKay (eds.), *The Norton Anthology: African American Literature* (New York and London, W. W. Norton & Co., 1997).

Baldwin, James, *The Fire Next Time* (London, Penguin, 1964).

Barton, Mukti, *Scripture as Empowerment for Liberation and Justice: The Experience of Christian and Muslim Women in Bangladesh* (Bristol, University of Bristol, 1999).

—'I am Black and beautiful', *Black Theology: An International Journal*, vol. 2, no. 2 (London, Equinox Publishing Ltd., 2004).

Beckford, Robert, *Jesus is Dread* (London, Darton, Longman & Todd, 1998).

Beckles, Hilary, 'Columbus and the contemporary dispensation within the Caribbean' in Paul Grant and Raj Patel (eds.), *A Time to Act* (Birmingham, Racial Justice and The Black and Third World Theological Working Group, 1992).

Bevans, Stephen B., *Models of Contextual Theology* (Maryknoll, NY, Orbis Books, 1992).

Bhogal, Inderjit, 'Mind your language', *Methodist Recorder*, 15 February 2001.

Bible, The Holy, Authorised King James Version (London, William Collins Sons & Co. Ltd., 1954).

Black Theology in Britain: A Journal of Contextual Praxis, issue 1 (Sheffield, Sheffield Academic Press, 1998).

—issue 4 (Sheffield, Sheffield Academic Press, 2000).

Black Theology: An International Journal, vol. 2, no. 2 (London, Equinox Publishing Ltd., 2004).

Brierley, Peter, *The Tide is Running Out: What the English Church Survey Reveals* (London, Christian Research, 2000).

Bright, John, *A History of Israel* (London, SCM Press, 1972).

Brown Douglas, Kelly, *The Black Christ* (Maryknoll, NY, Orbis Books, 1994).

Byron, Gay L., *Symbolic Blackness and Ethnic Difference in Early Christian Literature* (London and New York, Routledge, 2002).

Clutton-Brock, A., 'The English Bible' in V. F. Storr (ed.), *The English Bible: Essays by Various Authors* (London, Methuen & Co. Ltd., 1938), p. 78, cited in R. S. Sugirtharajah, *Postcolonial Criticism and Biblical Interpretation* (Oxford, Oxford University Press, 2002).

Cohen, Stanley, *States of Denial: Knowing about Atrocities and Suffering* (Cambridge, Polity Press, 2001).

Coleman, Kate, 'Black theology and Black liberation: a womanist perspective', *Black Theology in Britain: A Journal of Contextual Praxis*, issue 1 (Sheffield, Sheffield Academic Press, 1998).

Cone, Cecil, *The Identity Crisis in Black Theology* (Nashville, AMEC, 1975), p. 37, cited in Kelly Brown Douglas, *The Black Christ* (Maryknoll, NY, Orbis Books, 1994).

Cone, James H., *God of the Oppressed* (San Francisco, Harper & Row, 1975).

—*A Black Theology of Liberation*, 20th Anniversary edn. (Maryknoll, NY, Orbis Books, 1990).

—'Theology's great sin: silence in the face of White supremacy', *Black Theology: An International Journal*, vol. 2, no. 2 (London, Equinox Publishing Ltd., July 2004).

Cone, James H. and Wilmore, Gayraud S., *Black Theology: A Documentary History*, vol. 2 (Maryknoll, NY, Orbis Books, 1993).

Dalrymple, William, 'The incredible journey: did St Thomas found a church in South India? William Dalrymple unravels a Christian mystery' in Saturday Review, *Guardian*, 15 April 2000.

della Francesca, Piero (1416–92), 'Annunciation', a Fresco, in *The Holy Bible, Authorised King James Version* (London, William Collins Sons & Co. Ltd., 1954).

De Santa Ana, Julio, *Good News to the Poor: The Challenge of the Poor in the History of the Church* (Madras, The Christian Literature Society, 1978).

DiAngelo, Robin, 'Heterosexism: addressing internalized dominance', *Journal of Progressive Human Services*, vol. 8, no. 1, 1997.

Dixon, Lorraine, 'A reflection on Black identity and belonging in the context of the Anglican Church in England: a way forward', *Black Theology in Britain: A Journal of Contextual Praxis*, issue 4 (Sheffield, Sheffield Academic Press, 2000).

Doy, Gen, *Black Visual Culture: Modernity and Postmodernity* (London and New York, I. B. Tauris and Co. Ltd., 2000).

Edmead, Peter L., *The Divisive Decade: A History of Caribbean Immigration to Birmingham in the 1950s* (Birmingham, Birmingham Library Services, 1999).

Eze, Emmanuel Chukwudi, *Race and Enlightenment: A Reader* (Oxford, Blackwell, 1997).

Fabella, Virginia, and Lee Park, Sun Ai (eds.), *We Dare to Dream: Doing Theology as Asian Women* (Maryknoll, NY, Orbis Books, 1990).

Fanon, Frantz, *The Wretched of the Earth*, trans. Constance Farrington (London, Penguin Books, 1967).

—*Black Skin, White Masks*, trans. Charles Lam Markmann (London, Pluto Press, 1986).

Felder, Cain Hope (ed.), *The Original African Heritage Study Bible* (Tennessee, The James C. Winston Publishing Co., 1993).

Ferber, Abby L., 'What White supremacists taught a Jewish scholar about identity' in Margaret L. Anderson and Patricia Hill Collins (eds.), *Race, Class and Gender: An Anthology* (London, International Thomson Publishing Europe, 1998).

Findlay, Barbara, *With All of Who We Are: A Discussion of Oppression and Dominance* (Vancouver, Lazara Press, 1991).

Freire, Paulo, *Pedagogy of Hope: Reliving Pedagogy of the Oppressed*, trans. Robert R. Barr (New York, Continuum, 1994).

—*Pedagogy of the Oppressed*, trans. Myra Bergman Ramos (London, Penguin, 1996).

Fryer, Peter, *Staying Power: The History of Black People in Britain* (London, Pluto Press, 1984).

Gates, Jr, Henry Louis, and McKay, Neille Y. (eds.), *The Norton Anthology: African American Literature* (New York and London, W. W. Norton & Co., 1997).

Gee, Joshua, *The Trade and Navigation of Great-Britain Considered*, Sam. Buckley (1729).

Gibran, Kahlil, *The Prophet* (London, Heinemann, 1974).

Gill, Stephen, 'About the author' in Peter C. Mall, *Hamd-O-Sana* (Jalandhar, Peter's Publication, 1999).

Gjerding, Iben and Kinnamon, Katherine (eds.), *No Longer Strangers: A Resource for Women and Worship* (Geneva, WCC Publications, 1983).

Good News Bible with Apocrypha/Deuterocanonical Books (Glasgow, HarperCollins, 1993).

Gordon-Carter, Glynne, *An Amazing Journey: The Church of England's Response to Institutional Racism* (London, Church House Publishing, 2003).

Gottwald, Norman K. and Horsley, Richard A. (eds.), *The Bible and Liberation:*

Political and Social Hermeneutics (Maryknoll, NY, Orbis Books; London, SPCK, 1993).

Grant, Paul and Patel, Raj (eds.), *A Time to Speak* (Birmingham, Racial Justice and Black Theology Working Group, 1991).

—*A Time to Act* (Birmingham, Racial Justice and The Black and Third World Theological Working Group, 1992).

Grant, Paul, 'If it happened to you, tell me what would you do?' in Paul Grant and Raj Patel (eds.), *A Time to Speak* (Birmingham, Racial Justice and Black Theology Working Group, 1991).

Grenville, J., *The Collins History of the World in the Twentieth Century* (London, HarperCollins, 1994).

Hammad, Suheir, 'Untitled', cited in Rowan Williams, *Writing in the Dust: Reflections on 11th September and its Aftermath* (London, Hodder & Stoughton, 2002).

Haslam, David, *Race for the Millennium: A Challenge to Church and Society* (London, Church House Publishing, 1996).

—*The Churches and 'Race': A Pastoral Approach* (Cambridge, Grove Books, 2001).

Hobbs, Maurice, *Better will Come: A Pastoral Response to Institutional Racism in British Churches* (Nottingham, Grove Books, 1991).

Holy Bible: The New Revised Standard Version with Apocrypha (New York and Oxford, Oxford University Press, 1989).

Hwang, Hai Ok and Nguyen, Binh, 'Gathering ceremony', *In God's Image*, vol. 16, no. 4 (Kuala Lumpur, Asian Women's Resource Centre for Culture and Theology, 1997).

Insight Guide: The Dominican Republic and Haiti (Singapore Branch, Apa Publications Gmbh and Co. Verlag KG, 2000).

© Jarrett-Harvey, Vilma, 'Mother Land', 2004; 'Still I Rise', 2004.

© Johnson, Janet, 'The Reason Why', part 2, 2004; 'Contemporary Vibes', adapted from William Shakespeare's Hamlet, 2004; 'What is Truth?' 1998; 'Sometimes Saying "I'm Sorry" Is not Enough: A Tribute to Stephen Lawrence', 1998; 'African Queens', 1998; 'To be Black is Beautiful', 1998.

© Jones, Linda/CAFOD, 'A Healing Touch'.

Kasimbayan, 'Untitled' in Sharon Rose Joy Ruiz-Duremded (ed.), *Unleashing the Power Within Us: Meditations for Asian Women* (Quezon City, National Council of Churches in the Philippines, 2001).

Keller, Mary, 'Raced and gendered perspectives: towards the epidermalization of subjectivity in Religious Studies theory' in Ursula King and Tina Beattie, *Gender, Religion and Diversity, Cross-Cultural Perspectives* (London and New York, Continuum, 2004).

Kelly, Tony, 'The Bail Race is a Rat Race Not Fit for the Human Race', a masters degree dissertation in Socio-legal Studies (Birmingham, Birmingham University, 1991).

King, Jr, Martin Luther, 'Letter from Birmingham City Jail' in James M. Washington (ed.), *A Testament of Hope: The Essential Writings of Martin Luther King, Jr* (San Francisco, Harper & Row, 1986).

—'The American dream', *Negro History Bulletin*, vol. 31 (May 1968).

King, Ursula, and Beattie, Tina, *Gender, Religion and Diversity, Cross-Cultural Perspectives* (London and New York, Continuum, 2004).

Kinukawa, Hisako, 'The Syrophoenician woman: Mark 7.24–30' in R. S.

Sugirtharajah, *Voices from the Margin: Interpreting the Bible in the Third World*, revised edn (London, SPCK, 1995).

Kyung, Chung Hyun, *Struggle to be the Sun Again: Introducing Asian Women's Theology* (London, SCM Press, 1991).

—'"Han-pu-ri": doing theology from Korean women's perspective' in Virginia Fabella and Sun Ai Lee Park (eds.), *We Dare to Dream: Doing Theology as Asian Women* (Maryknoll, NY, Orbis Books, 1990).

Lamsa, George M., *Holy Bible from the Ancient Eastern Text: George M. Lamsa's Translation from the Aramaic of the Peshitta* (New York, HarperCollins, 1968).

Lartey, Emmanuel Y., *In Living Colour: An Intercultural Approach to Pastoral Care and Counselling* (London, Cassell, 1997).

Lorde, Audre, *Sister Outsider: Essays and Speeches* (Freedom CA, Crossing, 1984).

Macpherson, Sir William, *The Stephen Lawrence Enquiry Report* (London, The Stationery Office, 1999).

McIntosh, Peggy, 'White privilege and male privilege: a personal account of coming to see correspondences through work in Women's Studies' in Margaret L. Anderson and Patricia Hill Collins (eds.), *Race, Class and Gender: An Anthology* (London, International Thomson Publishing Europe, 1998).

Mall, Peter C., *Hamd-O-Sana* (Jalandhar, Peter's Publication, 1999).

Manley, M., *History of West Indies Cricket* (London, Deutsch, 1988).

Marley, Bob, 'Redemption Song' in Nick Crispin (comp.), *Bob Marley: The Chord Songbook* (London, Wise Publications, 1999).

Martin, Clarice J., 'A chamberlain's journey and the challenge of interpretation for liberation' in Norman K. Gottwald and Richard A. Horsley (eds.), *The Bible and Liberation: Political and Social Hermeneutics* (Maryknoll, NY, Orbis Books; London, SPCK, 1993).

Methodist Recorder, 15 February 2001.

Moon, Cyris H. S., 'A Korean minjung perspective: the Hebrews and the Exodus' in R. S., Sugirtharajah (ed.), *Voices from the Margin* (London, SPCK, 1991).

Moore, Robert B., 'Racist stereotyping in the English language' in Margaret L. Anderson and Patricia Hill Collins (eds.), *Race, Class and Gender: An Anthology* (London, International Thomson Publishing Europe, 1998).

Negro History Bulletin, vol. 31 (May 1968).

Orwell, George, *Nineteen-Eighty Four* (Harmondsworth, Penguin, 1954; first pub. 1949).

© Palmer, Sharon, 'The Reality of Crime', 1995.

Parekh, Bhikhu *et al.*, *The Future of Multi-Ethnic Britain: The Parekh Report* (London, Runnymede Trust, 2000).

Patel, Raj, 'Why do Christians wear ties?' in Paul Grant and Raj Patel (eds.), *A Time to Speak* (Birmingham, Racial Justice and Black Theology Working Group, 1991).

Pearsall, Judy (ed.), *The New Oxford Dictionary of English* (Oxford, Clarendon Press, 1998).

Pitts, Eve, 'Black womanist ethic' in Paul Grant and Raj Patel (eds.), *A Time to Speak* (Birmingham, Racial Justice and Black Theology Working Group, 1991).

Reddie, Anthony G., *Faith Stories and the Experience of Black Elders: Singing the Lord's Song in a Strange Land* (London, Jessica Kingsley Publishers, 2001).

Ruiz-Duremded, Sharon Rose Joy (ed.), *Unleashing the Power within Us: Meditations for Asian Women* (Quezon City, National Council of Churches in the Philippines, 2001).

Sartre, Jean-Paul, 'Preface' in Frantz Fanon, *The Wretched of the Earth*, trans. Constance Farrington (London, Penguin, 1967).

Slee, Nicola, 'Veneration of the Cross', in Nicola Slee, *Praying Like a Woman* (London, SPCK, 2004).

Seeds of Hope in the Parish Study Pack (Birmingham, Diocese of Birmingham, 1999).

Smith-Cameron, Ivor, *The Church of Many Colours* (London, Ivor Smith-Cameron, 1998).

Sugirtharajah, R. S. (ed.), *Voices from the Margin: Interpreting the Bible in the Third World*, revised edn (London, SPCK, 1995).

—*Postcolonial Criticism and Biblical Interpretation* (Oxford, Oxford University Press, 2002).

Tamez, Elsa, 'The scandalous message of James: the angle of praxis' in Norman K. Gottwald and Richard A. Horsley (eds.), *The Bible and Liberation: Political and Social Hermeneutics* (Maryknoll, NY, Orbis Books; London, SPCK, 1993).

Tutu, Desmond, *Hope and Suffering* (London, Fount Paperbacks, 1984).

Usry, Glenn and Keener, Craig S., *Black Man's Religion: Can Christianity be Afrocentric?* (Illinois, Inter Varsity Press, 1996).

Ward, Pete, *Youthwork and the Mission of God: Frameworks for Relational Outreach* (London, SPCK, 1997).

Washington, James M. (ed.), *A Testament of Hope: The Essential Writings of Martin Luther King, Jr* (San Francisco, Harper & Row, 1986).

Weems, Renita J., 'Womanist reflections on biblical hermeneutics' in James H. Cone and Gayraud S. Wilmore, *Black Theology: A Documentary History*, vol. 2 (Maryknoll, NY, Orbis Books, 1993).

Wild Goose Worship Group, *Stages on the Way: Worship Resources for Lent, Holy Week and Easter* (Glasgow, Wild Goose Publications, 1998).

Wilkinson, John L., *The Church in Black and White* (Edinburgh, St Andrew, 1993).

Williams, Delores S., *Sisters in the Wilderness: The Challenge of Womanist God-Talk* (Maryknoll, NY, Orbis Books, 1993).

Williams, Rowan, *Writing in the Dust: Reflections on 11th September and its Aftermath* (London, Hodder & Stoughton, 2002),

Wink, Walter, *Engaging the Powers* (Minneapolis, Fortress Press, 1992).

Websites

2001 Census. Available from http://www.birmingham.gov.uk/Generate Content?CONTENT_ITEM_ID=26205&CONTENT_ITEM_TYPE=0&MENU_ID=12672&EXPAND=11333

Acts of the Holy Apostle Thomas. Available from http://www.ccel.org/fathers2/ANF-08/anf08-99.htm

Apostle St Thomas in India. Available from http://members.tripod.com/~Berchmans/apostle.html and http://www.indianchristianity.org/thomas.html

Archbishop Desmond Tutu's Lecture. Available from http://www.episcopalchurch.org/3577_20571_ENG_HTM.htm

Bible Commentary. Available from http://www.crosswalk.ecom

Columbus and Western Civilization by Howard Zinn. Available from http://www.geocities.com/howardzinnfans/CDay.html

Commerce in the Bible, Israel – Crossroads of the East by Clarence H. Wagner, Jr.

Available from http://www.bridgesforpeace.com/publications/dispatch/
everydaylife/Article-28.html

Diversity, Social Cohesion and Opportunity: The Asian Example. Available from
http://www.article13.com/A13_ContentList.asp?strAction=GetPublication&
PNID=640 (as retrieved, 27 October 2004, 10:08:41 GMATT)

Don't Call Me Asian by Sarfraz Manzoor. Available from http://www.dawn.
com/2005/01/12/int14.htm

Early Christianity in Britain. Available from http://www.britainexpress.com/
History/Early_Christian_Britain.htm

East of the Euphrates: Early Christianity in Asia by T. V. Philip. Available from
http://www.religion-online.org/showchapter.asp?title=1553&C=1364

Fertile Crescent. Available from http://www.geocities.com/CapitolHill/
Parliament/2587/fc.html

Gibson goes for shock value over substance by Christopher Kelly in *Fort Worth
Star-Telegram.* Available from http://www.philly.com/mld/philly/
entertainment/special_packages/passion_of_christ/8028323.htm?1c

*Government and police must engage communities to build a fairer criminal justice
system.* Available from http://www.homeoffice.gov.uk/n_story.asp?
item_id=991

Hate Symbols. Available from http://gbgm-umc.org/umw/anti-hate/
symbolsofhate.html

National Statistics: News Release. Available from http://www.statistics.
gov.uk/pdfdir/migr1104.pdf

Negro Spirituals: Songs of Survival. Available from http://www.jsfmusic.
com/Uncle_Tom/Tom_Article3.html

N-G-R, niger, negro 'nigger': the n word from divine to racist. Available from
http://community2.webtv.net/PAULNUBIAEMPIRE/TRACKINGAND/

Religion in India: Christianity, September 1995. Available from
http://atheism.about.com/library/world/AJ/bl_IndiaOtherChristianity.htm

Religion in Britain, and in the Rest of the UK. Available from http://www.
religioustolerance.org/uk_rel.htm

The Giles Fraser Column, 'Imperial Christianity', 6 October 2003. Available from
http://www.ekklesia.co.uk

Who are Free Methodists? Available from http://www.freemethodistchurch.org/
Sections/About%20Us/Basic%20Info/FAQs/What's%20A%20Free%20
Methodist.htm